D1263240

LATIN AMERICAN ARCHITECTURE SINCE 1945

LATIN AMERICAN ARCHITECTURE

SINCE 1945

BY HENRY-RUSSELL HITCHCOCK

THE MUSEUM OF MODERN ART   NEW YORK

Reprint Edition 1972   *Published for The Museum of Modern Art by Arno Press*

NA
702
.H5
1972

724.9 H674

Hitchcock, Henry
Russell

Latin American
architecture since
1945.

TRUSTEES OF THE MUSEUM OF MODERN ART

JOHN HAY WHITNEY, CHAIRMAN OF THE BOARD: HENRY ALLEN MOE, 1ST VICE-CHAIRMAN: PHILIP L. GOODWIN, 2ND VICE-CHAIRMAN: WILLIAM A. M. BURDEN, PRESIDENT: MRS. DAVID M. LEVY, 1ST VICE-PRESIDENT: ALFRED H. BARR, JR., MRS. ROBERT WOODS BLISS, STEPHEN C. CLARK, RALPH F. COLIN, MRS. W. MURRAY CRANE*, RENÉ D'HARNONCOURT, MRS. EDSEL B. FORD, A. CONGER GOODYEAR, MRS. SIMON GUGGENHEIM*, WALLACE K. HARRISON, JAMES W. HUSTED*, MRS. ALBERT D. LASKER, MRS. HENRY R. LUCE, RANALD H. MACDONALD, MRS. SAMUEL A. MARX, MRS. G. MACCULLOCH MILLER, WILLIAM S. PALEY, MRS. BLISS PARKINSON, MRS. CHARLES S. PAYSON, DUNCAN PHILLIPS*, ANDREW CARNDUFF RITCHIE, DAVID ROCKEFELLER, MRS. JOHN D. ROCKEFELLER, 3RD, NELSON A. ROCKEFELLER, BEARDSLEY RUML, PAUL J. SACHS*, JOHN L. SENIOR, JR., JAMES THRALL SOBY, EDWARD M. M. WARBURG, MONROE WHEELER

*HONORARY TRUSTEE FOR LIFE.

DEPARTMENT OF ARCHITECTURE AND DESIGN

ARTHUR DREXLER, CURATOR
MILDRED CONSTANTÍNE, ASSOCIATE CURATOR OF GRAPHIC DESIGN
GRETA DANIEL, ASSOCIATE CURATOR OF INDUSTRIAL DESIGN

MUSEUM COMMITTEE ON ARCHITECTURE

PHILIP C. JOHNSON, CHAIRMAN; PIETRO BELLUSCHI; PHILIP L. GOODWIN, WALLACE K. HARRISON

DABNEY LANCASTER LIBRARY
LONGWOOD COLLEGE
FARMVILLE, VIRGINIA 23901

© 1955 by the Museum of Modern Art, New York
Printed in the United States of America

Library of Congress Catalog Card Number 71-169304
ISBN 0-405-01563-1

CONTENTS

77-00078

PREFACE AND ACKNOWLEDGMENTS

This is the Museum's second survey of Latin American architecture. The first, directed in 1939 by Philip L. Goodwin, and with photographs by G. E. Kidder Smith, was concerned exclusively with architecture in Brazil. That exhibition and book called to our attention the remarkable vitality of a modern architecture developing along lines somewhat different from our own or from that of Europe. Since that date, and perhaps more especially since 1945, the extent of building not only in Brazil but throughout Latin America; the mature authority of such masters as, for example, Pani in Mexico and Costa and Niemeyer in Brazil; the arrival of many European architects; and the emergence of several younger talents trained in their own countries or in the United States, have produced an architecture of such considerable range as to make desirable a detailed survey of its accomplishments.

To make this survey the Museum's International Program, directed by Porter McCray, commissioned Henry-Russell Hitchcock to visit eleven countries of Latin America. Mr. Hitchcock was accompanied by Rosalie Thorne McKenna, whose photographs of many of the buildings appear in this book, and whose stereo slides of the same buildings are also included in the exhibition.

Among the most important activities of the Museum's Department of Architecture and Design are exhibitions and publications which call attention to outstanding work in all countries. Such an exhibition was *Built in USA: Post-war Architecture*, which in 1953 presented a selection of the best American buildings since the close of World War II. For that project the Museum enjoyed, as it has many times in the past, the services of Henry-Russell Hitchcock, America's foremost historian of modern architecture. Assisted by an informally constituted panel of advisors, Mr. Hitchcock selected forty-three buildings in the United States for their "quality and significance of the moment."

Quality and significance of the moment still obtain as criteria, but the difference in scope between the two exhibitions required certain adjustments. It was not Mr. Hitchcock's intention to include every building of high quality. Generally the choice has favored examples most significant in the development of an individual architect's work. Significance of the moment has also another and somewhat wider meaning. Because the quantity of current Latin American building exceeds our own, the appearance there of predominantly "modern" cities gives us the opportunity to observe effects which we ourselves still only anticipate. Thus some buildings, or details of buildings, (as for example urban façades) have been included more for their part in an aggregate than for their stature as independent works of art. Where architectural forms are the result of social, economic, or technological conditions unfamiliar to North Americans, Mr. Hitchcock has explained the origin of those forms and their esthetic value.

It is through this informed evaluation of strictly architectural properties that Mr. Hitchcock conveys, I think, the quality and importance of architecture in Latin America.

On behalf of Henry-Russell Hitchcock the Museum wishes to thank the many architects represented in this book for having given generously their time and active cooperation, and the officials of the United States Embassies and the United States Information Service in Latin America for their interest and valuable help. The Museum most especially wishes to thank the following individuals whose advice and gracious assistance greatly facilitated the collection of material for the exhibition and book: Miss Claude Vincent, Miss Lota de Macedo Soares, Henrique Mindlin and Francisco Mattarazzo Sobrinho in Brazil; Mrs. Richard Loeb, Emilio Duhart, and Dr. Sergio Larrain in Chile; Dicken Castro in Colombia; Max Cetto in Mexico; Paul Linder in Peru; Carlos Raúl Villanueva and Moisés F. Benacerraf in Venezuela; and Dr. Jaime Benitez in Puerto Rico.

ARTHUR DREXLER

LATIN AMERICAN ARCHITECTURE SINCE 1945

Latin America extends for a continent and a half. Comparable in area to all Europe and Anglo-Saxon North America combined, it is, of course, not as thickly populated, since it includes very large areas of high mountains, deserts and jungles. Brazil, larger by all of Texas than the United States, has only some forty-five million inhabitants. But from Mexico City in North America, whose size has tripled in fifteen years, to Caracas, which positively seems to expand under the visitor's eye, the tremendous rate of population growth (3 per cent a year — double the rate in the rest of the world) and the increasing vitality of the local economy, have induced a rate of building production unequalled elsewhere in the Western World. Today, Mexico City and Rio de Janeiro are both much larger than Rome; and of the six largest cities in the Western Hemisphere, four are in Latin America.

That there is some connection between quantity and quality in architecture no one can deny, even if the mechanics of the relationship are mysterious. Not all building booms produce moments of distinction, and Le Corbusier's splendid Unité d'Habitation has risen in a post-war France where there has been little new construction. But in most Latin American countries today there is both quantity and quality in architecture.

The new architecture of Latin America belongs specifically to the age of the airplane. Until well into the twentieth century one of the principal characteristics of Latin America was its remoteness, not only from the rest of the Western world but, if the phrase may be pardoned, remoteness from itself. Spain administered her colonies through several viceregal capitals, each more closely linked to Madrid than to the others. Independence, coming gradually through nearly a century, brought not unity, as with the thirteen colonies in North America, but still greater separation, which to this day finds expression in debated borderlands and minor wars. No general Civil War, no transcontinental railroad system provided the nineteenth century either sentiment for or the physical possibility of closer union. Indeed, the railroad age never came to maturity nor was it followed by any age of the automobile. Horse and ship — ocean liner or river boat — remained the principal means of communication until the coming of the airplane. Today, there is perhaps no part of the world where air traffic is so vital, bringing all the South American countries into close contact with the outside world and, almost more significantly, with each other. Building materials rarely travel by air, but most architects do and their ideas as well. The São Paulo airport is the third busiest in the world, seventy flights a day linking it with Rio de Janeiro alone; and appropriately the Santos Dumont Airport at Rio de Janeiro, perhaps the most beautiful in the world and certainly the most conveniently located, is one of the two major buildings that called attention to the development of a brilliant Cariocan school of modern architecture.

The eyes of the world were first focused on Latin America during World War II. By 1942, when the Museum of Modern Art held its exhibition "Brazil Builds," it was evident that the previous five years had seen the creation of a new national idiom within the international language of modern architecture. The publication which accompanied that exhibition, with text by Philip L. Goodwin and photographs by G. E. Kidder Smith, presented the Brazilian achievement to the world at large. Nowhere was the achievement more of an inspiration than in the other countries of Latin America. Since that date, the professional periodicals of South America, led by the Brazilian review *Habitat,* and even more conspicuously and thoroughly by *L'Architecture d'Aujourd'hui* in France, the *Architectural Review* in England, *Domus* in Italy, and the *Architectural Forum* in this country, have provided recurrent reports on Brazilian architecture and a coverage somewhat less thorough of building activity in other Latin American countries. Particularly in the last five years it has become evident that the vitality of that activity was by no means limited to Brazil; the University Cities of Mexico City and Caracas, in particular, have attracted wide attention from the general as well as the professional press.

This volume aims to illustrate by a selected group of buildings from ten countries and one American dependency — the Commonwealth of Puerto Rico — the wide range of notable architecture that is being produced in the middle of the twentieth century throughout Latin America. It is, in one sense, a parallel or pendant to the volume *Built in U.S.A.: Post-War Architecture* prepared by the Museum three years ago. It will be found, I believe, to exceed that exhibition in variety of interest and at least to equal it in the average level of the work included. In certain fields, notably university cities and public housing, the United States in recent years has had little to offer as extensive in scope or as brilliant in design as the best Latin American work. In other fields, individual private houses for example, the very different climatic and psychological conditions — even though they vary in Latin America at least as much as they do in different parts of the U.S. — make direct comparison more difficult. Surprisingly enough, it is not in the field of tall urban buildings, where the lack of structural steel restricts height in the countries to the south, but in that of ecclesiastical construction, that the United States seems most definitely to lead in variety and quality of production in the post-war years. Apartment houses are a relative novelty in Latin America, at least outside of Buenos Aires and Rio, yet only in Chicago is the level of the best in the United States equal to the level of the best in the South.

The lands where this major flowering of modern architecture has taken place in the last twenty years are not unknown to the history of architecture. Particularly in Mexico and in the Andean highlands great prehistoric cultures have left behind monuments comparable to those of Egypt or Mesopotamia. In Mexico, at least, awareness of the Indian heritage forms an active element in the ideology of certain modern architects. (Diego Rivera, with characteristic extremism, has said indeed that the *frontons* or handball courts at the University City are the only really *Mexican* structures there because their pyramidal shapes imitate in simplified form the Aztec pyramids.) Continuity with the prehistoric past, varying enormously between different countries both in its reality and in its cultural significance, may better be brought up when discussing those countries where the concept has relevance.

In the colonial period, extending from the sixteenth century through the early nineteenth, the achievements of Latin America in general rival those of the Spanish and Portuguese homelands and have of late attracted the interest of various scholars in the United States. The richness of the architecture, especially in its more decorative aspects, and the curious flavor arising from the elaboration of various Renaissance and Baroque themes by Indian craftsmen, produced a series of style phases whose common qualities

ABOVE: PYRAMID OF THE SUN, TEOTIHUACÁN, MEXICO

ALTAR ROOM, MACHU PICCHU, PERU, C.1438-1532

14

ALBERTO T. ARAI: FRONTONS, UNIVERSITY CITY,
MEXICO, D.F., 1952

give the adjective "colonial" a far more precise meaning than it has with us.

The nineteenth- and early twentieth-century architecture of Latin America has been less studied than that of the prehistoric and colonial periods. French influence dominated the arts in Brazil, from the time Dom Pedro I in 1816 first imported a group of French artists and architects to give a properly imperial new start to the culture of his vast domain, and in Mexico at least from the time when Maximilian with Napoleon III's backing initiated a sort of Second Empire there in mid-century. Owing to a natural lag at so great a remove from Paris, the international Second Empire mode, elsewhere largely restricted to the third quarter of the century, seems in Latin America generally to have lasted until 1900. There followed a considerable effloresence of Art Nouveau, mostly in the Italian version known as *Stile Floreale*, but with originality almost worthy of Gaudí here and there, notably in the lush cultural climates of Havana and Rio.

After the first decade of the century and down to the acceptance of modern architecture — a date which varies considerably according to the degree of acceptance implied, but roughly 1935 in Brazil and perhaps as late as 1950 in certain other countries — there occurred, as quite generally elsewhere in the world, a recession. Perhaps the dictates of official French taste in architecture were nowhere (certainly not in France) as dominant as in most of Latin America. Even today in the more southerly countries one may see private mansions and larger edifices still going up that appear to be based on projects from the Paris ateliers of a generation ago. With this belated expression of the realm of the Ecole des Beaux Arts, South America better than North America might have justified the subtitle of Jacques Gréber's book on the architecture of the United States, "preuve de la force d'expansion du génie français." There also came in big city buildings an influence from the New York and Chicago of the same decades. At their least interesting, the centers of some Latin American cities resemble the centers of provincial Middle Western cities built up between 1910 and 1930. It is obvious that in many technical aspects Latin American architecture today owes a great deal, both good and bad, to the United States' standards of plumbing and elevators on the one hand, for example, and on the other, alas, to the congestion which arises from building tall structures in urban centers designed for the traffic of two or three hundred years ago. House planning, also, has been much influenced by North American practice, but there are many local conditions

16

which make major characteristics of the twentieth-century house as we know it in the United States impractical to the South, at least for the present.

Neither the nineteenth century nor the early twentieth seems to have produced important autochthonous developments. It is obvious though that many characteristics, some of Iberian origin, some developed locally in the colonial period, continued to color the local production — and I use the word color advisedly, since the exploitation of color is one of the most conspicuous of these — despite the contemporary European influences that dominated more formal architecture. One is always blindest to the achievements of the period immediately preceding one's own, but it would seem no exaggeration to state that Latin America has produced no Wright, no Perret, no Behrens. The late Uruguayan architect Julio Vilamajó, known in the United States as one of the two South Americans on the United Nations Building Commission, produced work of distinction and also headed a school of architecture at Montevideo which was the most advanced in Latin America. For the most part the "grand old men" of Latin America are in their fifties and still actively engaged both in production and in architectural education. It is significant that in several cases these older men are themselves products of the Ecole des Beaux Arts in Paris or of the local school of Bellas Artes which followed — and indeed still follow — the Paris pattern. But men such as José Villagran García in Mexico, Sergio Larrain in Chile, Lucio Costa in Brazil and Carlos Villanueva in Venezuela, in the last three decades led the profession out of the cul-de-sac of official French architecture and, in the case of Costa and Villanueva, are themselves responsible for some of the most brilliant current work as well as serving disinterestedly to assign important commissions to able and well-trained younger men.

The private collections of paintings of certain of these men and, in the case of Villanueva, the major commissions given to leading modern artists from the outside world such as Calder and Léger and Arp, reveal their cosmopolitan sympathies. The Paris they studied in a generation ago was not just the Paris of the Ecole but also the Paris which was the international capital of modern art. It is not surprising, therefore, that modern architecture when it came to Latin America should have had from the first a Latin and even a French accent, and that Le Corbusier himself should have been a consultant on the Ministry of Education and Public Health in Rio on which Oscar Niemeyer, Affonso Reidy and Jorge Moreira, among the present

17

NAVE OF CHURCH, SEMINARY OF SAN MARTÍN, TEPOTZOTLÁN, MEXICO,
EIGHTEENTH CENTURY

OPPOSITE: JOSÉ PEREIRA AROUCA: CHURCH OF ROSARIO DOS PRETOS, OURO
PRETO, MINAS GERAIS, BRAZIL, 1785

18

leaders of Brazilian architecture, assisted Costa in the late 1930s.

No European of established reputation, no Mies or Gropius or Mendelsohn settled in Latin America as they did in the United States. But Spaniards, like Félix Candela in Mexico and Antonio Bonet in Argentina; Mario Bianco in Peru, and José Delpini in Argentina, have made a positive contribution, while Max Cetto and Paul Linder, fleeing like Gropius, Mies and Mendelsohn from the Nazi regime, are among the most respected professionals in Mexico and Peru respectively. In Puerto Rico one of the chief architects is Henry Klumb, a German pupil of Frank Lloyd Wright, and in Venezuela Don Hatch from the United States is a leading practitioner. But despite the prominence of certain structures designed by North American architects — Harrison and Abramovitz's Embassies in Rio and Havana, Edward Stone's El Panamá hotel in Panama and his enormous hospital in Lima still in construction, Holabird and Root's Tequendama hotel in Bogotá and Lathrop Douglas' Creole Oil Building in Caracas — the major contribution of the United States has been of a different and less direct order.

The excellent school at Montevideo formerly headed by Julio Vilamajó has been mentioned; as also (at least by implication) those headed by Villagran García at the National University of Mexico, and Larrain at the Catholic University of Santiago in Chile. But on the whole the Latin American schools are provincial at their best and laggardly Beaux Arts at their frequent worst. A very considerable proportion of the best Latin American architects, therefore, particularly those under forty, owe at least the final stages of their professional education to the architectural schools of the United States. It is not alone the more famous and old established schools or those that have been headed by world famous architects like Gropius and Mies, not just Harvard, Illinois Institute of Technology, Yale, Cornell, and Columbia, that have helped to form the architects of Latin America, but less internationally known schools such as the University of Michigan, Georgia Institute of Technology and the Universities of Oregon and Florida. There are many reasons why Latin America neither could nor should become too dependent in architecture, any more than in other ways, on the United States. The Iberian cultural background, the available — or more precisely the unavailable — building materials, the predominant climatic conditions, all help to explain why Latin American architecture will never be a provincial offshoot of that of the United States in the way it once was almost that of

France. It is a tribute to our schools that they have given to Latin Americans a training so broad that it could readily be applied under very different local conditions. Even the influences of the great masters, Wright and Gropius and Mies, are rarely very noticeable; which is the more surprising since no single Latin American architect as yet, except Niemeyer, has established so sharply personal a style that his influence on his colleagues is worthy of comment. In a sense, there is in present day Latin America — outside Brazil and Mexico at least — something approaching Gropius' ideal of an impersonal anonymous architecture. Even national characteristics are often better explained by different climatic conditions or different materials and methods of construction than by deeper cultural currents.

At the expense of over-simplification it will be well, therefore, before proceeding to characterize the production of the various countries and leading individual architects to make a few statements concerning the characteristics of the Latin American architectural scene as a whole. Despite the enormous range of longitude on either side of the equator, the variety of climatic conditions in the most heavily populated areas is perhaps less than in the United States. Because so many of the principal cities are located high in the mountains — for example, Caracas at 3,000 feet, Mexico City at 7,500, Bogotá at 8,000 — altitude affects their climate and the dominant character is warm-temperate rather than hot-tropical. Outside the Caribbean area, the major seaboard cities, such as Rio, Montevideo, Buenos Aires and Lima, are far enough south of the equator so that they also, except in midsummer, are not characteristically tropical. Nevertheless, in the greater part of Latin America the sun creates problems both of heat and glare unfamiliar in much of the northern hemisphere and having a profound effect on architecture.

There is an even more notable homogeneity in the building materials and methods throughout Latin America, best explained by what is almost completely, or very generally, lacking. Except to a small extent in Mexico, Latin America produces no structural steel and is unable, or at any rate disinclined, to import it. In the countries near the equator superb cabinet woods exist in profusion, but nowhere is there the supply of structural timber on which so much of the building industry in the United States depends. Here the old tradition of masonry construction and, one supposes, the lack of skill at carpentry, combine with the unavailability of timber to make wooden construction, at least in the most heavily populated areas, almost unknown.

CÂNDIDO PORTINARI: MURAL OF *AZULEJOS* (PAINTED TILES) ON GYMNASIUM OF THE PRIMARY SCHOOL BY AFFONSO EDUARDO REIDY, RUA CAPITÃO FÉLIX, RIO DE JANEIRO, BRAZIL, 1948-50

22

Yet building stones also seem to be lacking and marbles or other natural facing materials are generally inferior, if local, and obviously expensive and cumbersome to import. In looking closely at the buildings of what may be called the Beaux-Arts period, extending from the middle of the last century down to some ten years ago (and to the present in more laggard areas) it is a recurrent surprise to find that what appears to be limestone is almost always skillfully modeled stucco. Even burned clay building materials, bricks and structural tiles, although used everywhere, are in most countries so inferior that it is awkward practically and visually to leave them exposed. On the one hand, therefore, one may see wall surfaces apparently of brick that are actually of deceptively scored and painted stucco; on the other hand, where real bricks are used they must ordinarily be oiled or varnished to make them impenetrable to moisture.

Thus it is that the characteristic and almost exclusive building material is concrete, reinforced in various ways, the structural shell filled in with rubble or more usually with low-grade tile or brick and covered with painted stucco. In the pre-Inca ruins of Peru at Pachecamac near Lima, built of mud-brick, one may see patches of the original painted rendering and so realize that painted stucco or its equivalent has been in local use for several millennia. Where the climate is very dry as at Lima, painted stucco surfaces, from the 1920s characteristic of so much European modern architecture, stand up very well. In damper seaboard cities such as Rio de Janeiro they are less satisfactory. Everywhere, architects have been seeking more permanent surfacing materials, natural or artificial; and in the last few years mosaic either of glass — originally imported from Italy — or of glazed tile has had a tremendous success. There is little of the Wrightian feeling for the "nature of materials" in Latin America and it is argued that mosaic is merely a form of permanent paint. Mosaic certainly has its uses in regions where polychromy is an old local tradition never canceled out in popular building by the monochromatic modes of nineteenth-century Paris. But one may query the casualness with which it is applied, particularly over squared corner members, and the frequent violence of the color effects. An older Iberian tradition revived fairly generally in the last two decades is the covering of walls with *azulejos* or painted tiles, characteristically but not necessarily blue and white as their name implies. These may be of conventional patterns, repeated over a broad area almost like a sort of external wallpaper, or large

JULIO VILAMAJÓ: FACULTY OF
ENGINEERING, UNIVERSITY
OF THE REPUBLIC, 565 JULIO
HERRERA Y REISSIG AVENUE,
PARQUE RODO, MONTEVIDEO,
URUGUAY, 1937

EDWARD STONE: EL PANAMÁ
HOTEL, PANAMA CITY,
PANAMA, 1950

ABOVE: JOSÉ DELPINI: S.I.T. SPINNING SHED, PILAR, ARGENTINA, 1949-50

FÉLIX CANDELA: WAREHOUSE IN CONSTRUCTION, INSURGENTES NORTE, MEXICO, D.F., 1954

compositions especially designed by well-known painters to provide focal points of interest. Similar compositions executed in glass or tile mosaic are also frequently used, and in Mexico various natural rocks have been utilized to produce surfaces of a more rugged and architectural character that are hardly less brilliant and varied in color.

The many devices inherited or newly developed to control the excessive heat and glare of the sun, the very considerable use of color — itself probably related to the light conditions which tend to make white buildings painfully glaring — are among the physical factors that give Latin American architecture its general consistency of character and differentiate it from that of the United States or Europe, quite as much as do the general lack of steel and timber for structural use and the lack of satisfactory brick and structural tile.

The use of ferro-concrete, while generally conventional enough, has encouraged, as in southern Europe, the exploitation of shell vault forms. These are frequently designed by engineers of Spanish or Italian training. There is less of this sort of construction in fact than the outside world has assumed, but from the paraboloid vaults of Enrique de la Mora's and Niemeyer's churches to the ingenious industrial roofs of Candela, there is much of this nature which cannot be matched in the United States. Perhaps there still exists, in countries which have a tradition of masonry vaulting, more innate sympathy for the vault-like shapes of shell concrete construction. But certainly the lack of structural steel and timber all but forces such solutions where wide spans are needed and encourages their substitution for flat slabs even in small-scale construction. Curved skylines such as segmental and paraboloid forms produce are far more common than elsewhere in the world. Even in plan, the curve is more frequently used in Latin America than in the United States and is a characteristic of the personal manner of Niemeyer. A certain lyricism — of which color and curved forms are both important ingredients without being by any means universal — seems to have a continuous appeal to the Iberian temperament. It is hard nevertheless to point to much continuity of feeling between the incredibly sumptuous ecclesiastical architecture of both the Spanish and the Portuguese colonies and the generic severity of the modern architecture even as it has developed in Latin America.

Architecture, even in modern times, is much affected by psychological as well as by material factors. At first thought Latin America, by the very name we apply to it, might be assumed to be more of a piece ethnically, and hence psychologically, than is in fact the case. While the earliest European settlers in the area almost all came from the Iberian peninsula, the Spanish and the Portuguese strains are by no means identical. The history of Brazil, through much of the last century the seat of an autochthonous empire of which the home country became for a while a mere appendage, is not parallel to that of the various Spanish colonies which obtained their freedom in that period from Madrid. Common to almost the entire area are the indigenous Indian populations. The extent of their intermixture with those of European stock and — far more significantly — the attitude of enthusiasm for or denigration of the Indian heritage, varies greatly. Only in Mexico is there a conscious preoccupation with retaining continuity in modern national culture with the Indian as well as with the Iberian past. In Brazil and around the Caribbean the Negro element in the population, whose degree of assimilation varies a great deal, is as important statistically as the Indian, but probably has little relevance to architecture. But from colonial times European immigrants of non-Iberian origin have played an important role in other parts of Latin America. In Brazil, particularly, but almost as much in Argentina, Germans and Italians (not to speak of other, smaller, groups of non-American origin) play a vital part in the life of the community and not least in architecture. In São Paulo, for example, of the two leading architects, one is of Italian and the other of German descent, while two of the most successful are respectively first-generation Polish and French. Architects of Italian birth are among the leaders in Columbia and Peru, and German architects are well-established in Mexico and Peru. Only one architect from the United States plays a prominent part in the scene, Don Hatch in Caracas. But the visitor from the north cannot help being struck by the fact that a leading Argentinian architect is named Williams and a leading Uruguayan is named Jones, although both their families have been settled in Latin America for generations. In varying degree, however, most of the non-Iberians, whether they or their ancestors emigrated to the New World, have ultimately been assimilated more completely than the European architects who settled in the United States just before the last war.

The major element of cultural homogeneity is provided by the Catholic Church. There are, of course, some Protestants, and in certain areas large groups of Jews. And in the realm of ideology many are lukewarm in their acceptance of the Church. Catholic intellectuals among the architects, for example, are more than over-balanced by Communist ones outside of Mexico. But the Church, great and almost exclusive patron of architecture in the Colonial period, is laggard at building today and generally unresponsive to new ideas. There are probably more Catholic churches of current architectural interest in the predominantly Protestant United States than in all of Latin America. The best-known modern church, Niemeyer's São Francisco at Pampulha (page 64), completed ten years ago, has never been consecrated by the bishop; and the most interesting later church was built by a German disciple of Frank Lloyd Wright (page 70).

But if the Church has little direct effect on architecture and refuses in general to employ the leading modern architects, it has a powerful indirect influence. The very large families, balanced in most countries by large staffs of servants, have discouraged apartment building and require in house-planning what seems to North American eyes a curious imbalance between the living and the sleeping and service areas. Other potent influences on domestic architecture are Iberian rather than specifically Catholic. The degree of seclusion demanded varies from country to country, from Mexican houses enclosed with their high and unbroken walls to Niemeyer's glazed pavilion at Gávea. But almost everywhere the openings must be grilled or otherwise protected to keep out thieves and the houses tend to open inward on a patio rather than outward onto a lawn. On the other hand, there are strong and growing North American influences in domestic architecture and open planning is often specifically like that of the newest houses of the United States as well as generically modern.

Considering the very large numbers of Latin American architects who have at least completed their professional education in the United States and the familiarity with North American production provided by both the local and imported professional magazines, as well as by exhibitions, it is surprising that there is not more influence from the United States. This speaks for the solidity of the local cultural tradition, whether that be considered in itself a good thing or a bad one. North American influence is most evident in the centers of the cities. There the tall new office buildings, rising too often in narrow streets laid out in the sixteenth century, produce, with only a minimum of traffic, congestion as serious as that in North American cities. Only in Caracas are urbanistic steps being taken of an order comparable to the problem. Elsewhere, as in the States, ameliorative measures in the way of new and wide streets barely keep pace with building construction. Too often, for lack of adequate control, the biggest buildings continue to go up in the old central districts and not on the wide new avenues.

But if the tall business buildings are generically North American — and the skyscrapers rise thicker today in Mexico City or São Paulo than in most cities of the United States — their level of quality is surprisingly high even though ferro-concrete construction, with only a few impractical exceptions, limits heights to under twenty stories. The problems of sun control have produced a variety of interesting façade treatments, so that the vocabulary of commercial architecture is considerably more varied than with us. Moreover, the bulk of building in the post-war years is proportionately so much greater than in most of the United States that the flavor of city after city strikes the casual visitor, even more perhaps than the specialist, as being more modern than anything but a Houston or a Miami Beach at home.

Architecture is still very much an art in Latin America. The articulate elements in the community (a far smaller proportion than in the United States because of the enormous disparity in numbers between the very small ruling class and the masses of Indian peons) expect more from architects than purely "functional" solutions. Public authorities in particular clearly turn to architecture as a principal expression of cultural ambition. In the more southerly countries, conservative taste still demands and obtains from architects private mansions of a French Beaux-Arts order of forty years ago. But public buildings for government use more often than not are strikingly contemporary, if only rarely strikingly excellent in design. Hospitals and schools are generally less bold but are sounder in design. Most notably evidencing the high standards of official taste are the public housing projects and the University Cities, both clear expressions of the sociological and cultural aspirations of the various presidents and their regimes. Construction often lags in these fields, but the determination to achieve monumental results is evident in almost every Latin American country. To some extent this determination is self-defeating. More modest educational plants, carried out piecemeal over the years, might serve the current needs of higher education more efficiently. But certainly the scope and the homogeneity of these projects, whether they are the work of teams of architects as in Mexico, or of single men as in Rio and Caracas, is shaming to North Americans even if we remember Wright's Florida Southern Campus.

Although in the last few years it is the University City of Mexico that has received the most publicity, in part because Mexico City is visited by so many travelers from the United States, Brazil, whose new architecture was the first to focus attention on Latin America, remains the country with the most solidly established modern tradition and provides the greatest number of individual buildings of distinction. As the Brazilian Villa-Lobos is the best known of Latin American composers, so Niemeyer is certainly the architect whose fame is justifiably greatest. But Brazilian modern architecture does not stand or fall by the work of the man Gropius has called its "bird of paradise." When the Ministry of Education and Public Health, still perhaps the finest single modern structure in Latin America, was commissioned nearly twenty years ago, the team of architects in charge was led by Lucio Costa. It did not at first even include Niemeyer to whom Costa gives particular credit today for the building as it was finally designed. An older architect of French training, responsible through SPHAN (Serviço do Pâtrimonio Histórico e Artístico Nacional) for the meticulous restoration of so many of the monuments of the Brazilian past, Costa is more responsible than any one else for the creative turn which Brazilian architecture took in the late 1930s. At his suggestion, Vargas' Minister of Education, Gustavo Capanema, called Le Corbusier to Rio to prepare a general plan for a University City in the upper bay. Under Le Corbusier worked Costa and Niemeyer, and also Affonso Reidy. The University City now in construction is the work of Jorge Moreira, who was associated with Reidy and Niemeyer under Costa on the Ministry when it was begun in 1937. These men share with Niemeyer the credit, under Costa's leadership and with Le Corbusier's advice, for the Ministry and are thus properly to be considered co-founders of the Brazilian contemporary school. The painter Cândido Portinari and the landscape architect Roberto Burle-Marx were also associated on the Ministry commission. Ever since, it may almost be said, no major Brazilian building has been completed without the *azulejos* of Portinari and the gardens of Burle-Marx. It is evident that these men all shared in the formation of the new architecture and joined in inventing its most characteristic formal features. Low paraboloid shell vaults, in-sloping "butterfly" roofs, out-sloping building façades, various types of grill and louver-work for sun control were all developed in common — and not, as is sometimes supposed because of the greater fame of his work, borrowed from Niemeyer.

If the Ministry remains the finest modern building in Brazil, it is never-theless far from being a typical one. Although the interiors are in bad shape owing to the almost incredible Brazilian negligence in the maintenance of public buildings, it is generally better built than other new work in Rio. One wonders whether it is cost or the general Carioca preference for lighter and gayer coloring that explains why the handsome mottled gray gneiss which was used for much of the exterior surface — as well as for the trim — of many Colonial and later buildings in Rio, has never been employed again. The *azulejos* by Portinari (alas, fallen away here and there by now) and the vividly colored tile mosaic of the curved constructions of the roof, as well as the "free-form" Burle-Marx gardens on the roofs (gardens which without proper maintenance become scraggy jungles whose original design is hard to make out) have all been used over and over again, although rarely with the discretion shown here.

The later work of Costa, Reidy and Moreira included in this volume bal-ances that of Niemeyer and illustrates the range of the Carioca school of architects. Reidy is almost more Corbusian than Niemeyer if with less per-sonal lyricism. Costa's apartment blocks, Italian more than Corbusian, with their charming pale colors, varied grill work, and general directness of design and delicacy of scale, make one regret that he has built so little, effac-ing himself consciously beside the greater brilliance of the younger associate he first set going. Moreira's somewhat comparable apartment house, quieter and more restrained even than Costa's and his Instituto de Puericultura at the Cidade Universitaria, whose almost un-Brazilian qualities of refined under-statement and perfect execution in detail promise well for the large schools of architecture and engineering — and the Polyclinic Hospital now rising toward completion nearby — display a disciplined talent capable of heading distinguished teamwork in a large government architectural office.

While the Ministry was rising in Rio, and Costa and Niemeyer in asso-ciation with Paul Lester Wiener were displaying in the Brazilian Pavilion at the New York World's Fair of 1939 a full-fledged example of the new Brazilian architecture, two other architects, the brothers Mauricio and Milton Roberto, were designing and initiating at Rio what is still perhaps the most attractive airport in the world. The Santos Dumont Airport, long in con-struction and even today not entirely complete, occupies filled land in the bay at the edge of Rio's downtown section. Here, as in Costa's apartment

OPPOSITE: ROBERTO BURLE-MARX:
GARDEN FOR MME ODETTE MONTEIRO,
CORREIAS, PETRÓPOLIS, BRAZIL

LUCIO COSTA AND OTHERS (LE CORBUSIER, CONSULTANT):
MINISTRY OF EDUCATION AND PUBLIC HEALTH,
RIO DE JANEIRO, BRAZIL, 1937-42

32

MARCELO AND MILTON ROBERTO; LANDSCAPING BY ROBERTO BURLE-MARX:
SANTOS DUMONT AIRPORT, RIO DE JANEIRO, BRAZIL, 1940

OPPOSITE: GENERAL VIEW OF COPACABANA OCEAN FRONT,
RIO DE JANEIRO, BRAZIL

house, the feeling is more Italian than Corbusian, particularly inside where the ranges of white marble-sheathed piers supporting a pink ceiling produce a vast concourse of very great elegance. Unfortunately, as with so many modern buildings in Rio, the exterior has weathered badly, as painted stucco must in a seaside atmosphere, and the later practice, now ubiquitous, of covering buildings with mosaic, finds its justification.

In all the profusion of construction of the post-war years, a very large proportion of the buildings, even some by the best architects, already appears rather tawdry; and among all the apartment houses of the famous Copacabana district none is of the quality of Moreira's and Costa's elsewhere in the city. Fortunately the superb natural setting, the finest in the world, overpowers the architecture.

Good modern architecture in Brazil is by no means confined to the capital. Many other Brazilian cities contain works of merit, some by Carioca architects, others by local men. São Paulo is a metropolis hardly second to Rio and growing even more rapidly. A higher and dryer climate offers less difficult problems of surface maintenance and in general standards of execution seem to be higher both in terms of rate of production and of finish. Paulista architecture tends to be less specifically Brazilian in flavor than that of Rio, more sober in design and in color. The tremendous concentration of building activity creates an over-all picture more remarkable as a whole than are the individual ingredients. More than any other Latin American city São Paulo epitomizes the incredibly rapid transformation of the architectural scene in the last fifteen years, although it was a quite considerable twentieth-century city long before that.

Much that has been said earlier concerning Latin American architecture in general is particularly relevant to Brazil. Here we find the greatest variety of sun-screening devices, from permanent concrete *brise-soleils* to movable wooden jalousies and openwork screens of tile and precast concrete. Here are the earliest and on the whole the most successful examples of modern *azulejos* as also an epitome of the problems of more or less permanent colored surfacing materials in the absence of satisfactory local stone or good bricks. Here above all is the center of activity of the most intensely personal talent in architecture, Oscar Niemeyer, and the most direct evidence of his considerable influence. Against Niemeyer's lyricism there has been no sharp reaction. But the earlier attempts to outbid him in boldness of design and construction seem now to be balanced by a greater preoccupation with sound execution and readily maintainable surfaces. In the work of Moreira, Bratke and Bernardes, in different ways and in different degrees, a quieter and more disciplined elegance appears related ultimately to the work of Mies outside Latin America rather than to that of Le Corbusier.

The modern architecture of Colombia, except for the Stadium at Cartagena, has attracted much less attention than that of Brazil or Mexico, or most lately Venezuela. In many ways it stands apart from the architecture of the rest of Latin America as Bogotá, the capital, does by the relatively cool and wet climate provided by its great altitude. The cool temperament of the almost purely Northern-Spanish Colombians contrasts likewise with that of the more volatile Cariocas, and professional connections with the United States in architecture, as in other fields, have long been very close. Nowhere are there more architects whose training is North American and many of the characteristic problems they have faced are more familiar in North America than elsewhere in South America. With a less serious sun control problem than other Latin Americans, their soundly built business buildings would not look out of place in the cities of the northern United States, yet they would in many cases stand out by their clear and well organized design. The excellence of the technical standards of construction allow the use of exposed concrete elements, sometimes, as in the work of Violi, a pupil of Perret, handled with Perret's refinement of finish; sometimes, as in Cuellar, Serrano and Gómez university building, treated more simply and directly. Excellent brick, and in the case of the last-mentioned building, exposed building tile, provide, on occasion, surfaces that stand up well to the wet climate. The local sandstone, pleasant in color and graining, which has been much used in the last few years to provide surfacing slabs for large buildings is not weathering well and is now passing out of favor. Positive color effects are little favored in Colombia and the occasional introduction of *azulejos* tends to appear exotic.

In the short generation since flight linked it closely with the outside world Bogotá has grown too rapidly to cope in time with its urbanistic problems. A new wide avenue offers but limited alleviation of the traffic situation. The general increase in height of downtown buildings from the traditional two to fifteen or so, however excellent the individual buildings, has created in the narrow sixteenth-century streets of the colonial grid plan the worst congestion

GENERAL VIEW OF DOWNTOWN SÃO PAULO, BRAZIL

BRUNO VIOLI: EDIFICIO SMIDT, CARRERA 7A,
BOGOTÁ, COLOMBIA, 1951

ARANJO AND MURTRA, LTDA.: SWIMMING POOL, COUNTRY CLUB, BOGOTÁ, COLOMBIA, 1951

in Latin America. The residential area spreads more openly along the base of the mountains and the newer houses, together with two country clubs lying further out, create a succession of suburban developments rather Californian in type. Nearer the old city apartment houses and such row housing as "La Soledad" begin to provide middle-class dwellings of sound if uninspired design.

Somewhat apart from the general almost Anglo-Saxon character of Colombian architecture is that of the work done with shell concrete construction in stadiums, hippodromes, industrial plants, and even in houses. But except for the unfinished church of Our Lady of Fatima, two chapels at the Gimnasio Moderno and the Cavalry School by Moya (who was trained partly at the Cranbrook Academy, it is interesting to note, but is more Mexican in the tense emotionalism of his architecture) there is a general impression of sobriety in design and sound technique even in relatively experimental types of construction. The practice, common throughout Latin America, of combining construction firms with architectural partnerships, partly explains this and is seen at its best in the production of Cuellar, Serrano and Gómez.

I have said that the quality of Moya's ecclesiastical work is somewhat Mexican. Especially in the use of paraboloid shell vaults he seems closer to Enrique de la Mora's Church of La Purísima in Monterrey, the earliest designed (1939) of all the buildings included in this book. In Mexico the extensive use of shell construction, particularly in industrial work, by the Spanish-born engineer Félix Candela is particularly interesting. Because of their somewhat unarchitectural nature Candela's own factories and warehouses do not fall properly within the scope of this selection, but the Ciba laboratories which he built as contracting engineer for the architect Alejandro Prieto illustrate some of his characteristic concrete "umbrellas."

The Mexican architecture which has attracted the attention of every tourist from the North is, of course, that of the "skyscrapers" along the Avenida Juárez, the Paseo de la Reforma, and the Avenida Insurgentes, where a Los Angeles-like mid-twentieth-century skyline has been imposed over what was a largely Second Empire business and residential area. In general the tallest and most conspicuous of these skyscrapers are the poorest, stridently assertive in design and heavy in color. The best, on the other hand, notably those by Juan Sordo Madaleno, quieter in design and color, compare not unfavorably in interest, if perhaps not always in soundness of construc-

GENERAL VIEW OF THE PASEO DE LA REFORMA, MEXICO, D.F.

RAÚL IZQUIERDO, MARCELO AGUILAR: SCHOOL OF ENGINEERING AND ARCHITECTURE, INSTITUTO POLITÉCNICO NACIONAL, MEXICO, D.F., 1953

tion and excellence of finish, with those of Colombia, even if they lack the originality of those in Brazil. There are particular hazards in building tall structures in Mexico City since the curious terrain, produced by the Spaniards by filling in a lake, sinks irregularly a foot or two a year and complicated devices, such as adjustable piles, are only just being developed to take care of the situation. Needless to say uneven settlement combined with hasty construction produces problems of physical maintenance more serious than those of Rio. Surfacing buildings with violently colored glass mosaic, as in the last few years, is not even a palliative of the situation.

Almost as familiar as the large business buildings are those of the University City. Rather remote from the center of Mexico City for the convenience of professors and students, the University City occupies a magnificent site with lava formations in the foreground and a ring of mountains behind. It is with little question the most spectacular extra-urban architectural entity of the North American continent and has in scale and degree of completion no real rival in the rest of Latin America. On it collaborated very large numbers of architects and it requires consideration both as a whole and as several individual structures. Here bold color, architecturally scaled external mosaics, and a somewhat insensitive handling of the conventional elements of modern design, achieve a peculiarly Mexican intensity in which references to the Indian heritage, generally pictorial rather than architectural, play a positive role. But there are here quieter and more conventional modern structures such as Enrique de la Mora's Institute of Humanities and the Student Union, shadowed though they are by the aggressiveness of the taller structures such as the Administration Building, the Library and the buildings of the Faculties of Science and Medicine. This tremendous educational plant, superhuman to any eye in scale and inhuman in the distances to be traversed on foot by those who will use it, does include in its genteel layout, for which Pani and del Moral are particularly responsible, many fine spatial effects and generous transitions of plane from level to level. In detail — if one can call a mosaic covering the four walls of a tall library stack tower a detail — there is some of the boldest and also perhaps the most successful integration of two-dimensional art, and also of plastic art, with architecture. O'Gorman, painter as well as sculptor, conceived a library stack-tower almost as though it were merely the support for four enormous illustrated leaves from a codex. Yet his materials are architectural, being rough-surfaced

44

natural minerals rather than shiny glass mosaic, and so also is his scale. Natural minerals, but handled in relief, are also used in the figural decoration by Diego Rivera on the stadium — almost the only late work of his with any architectural quality.

In Mexican public housing, the large-scale organization of blocks of vary-ing height almost rivals in monumentality the University City. In the best example, the Centro Urbano Presidente Juárez, the collaboration of the painter Carlos Mérida has provided less strident polychromy and more archi-tectonic figural decoration. Unfortunately, in the field of hospital building, the projects for a sort of Medical City almost rivaling the University City seem to have bogged down some years ago. But on the other side of the city the extensive plant of the Instituto Politécnico advances rapidly toward com-pletion. It will be less typically Mexican, and more consistent in scale and design.

The modern houses of Mexico speak a rather different language than that of the downtown skyscrapers and the large complexes for which the State is the client. Here more than anywhere else in Latin America, the semi-oriental seclusion of Iberian tradition has been maintained. In the subdivision of Jardines de Pedregal, so handsomely laid out by Luis Barragán, one sees chiefly high blank walls of lava and one can hardly tell whether or not habita-tions exist behind them. Inside the high walls the whole area of the lot is likely to be made livable, indeed sometimes there will be no covered or enclosed living room, but only a patio or garden, often with the planting organized by Barragán. Insofar as one can distinguish the houses as roofed buildings from the walled complexes of which they form but a part, there is considerable variety of approach, from the traditional structure and heavy solid effects of Barragán's own house, based on local peasant ways of build-ing but highly sophisticated in its simplicity, to the Miesian lightness of Artigas' work. Granted the climate and the ways of living, these are among the most successful of Latin American houses, but as different as possible from most of the new houses of the States and unfortunately extremely diffi-cult to present adequately in photographs.

The newest area of architectural achievement in Latin America is Vene-zuela. In Caracas, the characteristic height of city buildings has risen from one to some twenty stories in about five years. At the University City, which more than rivals that of Mexico in the variety of its associated works of art —

MAX CETTO: HOUSE FOR THE ARCHITECT, CALLE DEL AGUA, JARDINES DEL PEDREGAL, MEXICO, D.F., 1948

FRANCISCO ARTIGAS: HOUSE FOR FEDERICO GÓMEZ, CALLE DEL RISCO 240, JARDINES
DEL PEDREGAL, MEXICO, D.F., 1952

OPPOSITE: LUIS BARRAGÁN: HOUSE FOR THE ARCHITECT, CALLE GENERAL FRANCISCO
RAMÍREZ 14, JARDINES DEL PEDREGAL, MEXICO, D.F., 1948

sculpture by Arp and Pevsner, mosaic and stained glass by Léger, a vast auditorium ceiling by Calder — the advance of Carlos Raúl Villanueva to a leading position in Latin America can easily be read. His Olympic Stadium and his Aula Magna with its attached Plaza Cubierta are among the most vigorous examples of modern architecture to be seen anywhere. Indeed to many, accustomed to associating Latin American architecture with the grace and lyricism of the Carioca architects, the vigor of Villanueva's exposed concrete may appear almost brutal. The organization of the University City, while more compact and human in scale than that of Mexico's, is less clear and geometrical.

Villanueva is also responsible for establishing the sound architectural traditions of the Banco Obrero, the local housing authority, although the latest work, both the middle-class apartment block at Cerro Grande and the almost unbelievably extensive operations at Cerro Piloto, is by Guido Bermúdez. In these the concrete is stuccoed and painted, still rather in the vein of the 1920s at Cerro Grande, but with more of the subtlety of the local polychrome tradition in the vast ranges of the blocks of Cerro Piloto.

The newest and tallest skyscraper in Caracas, the Edificio Polar, represents a less local tradition of modern design. With one of its architects a pupil of Mies van der Rohe, it is not surprising to find it quite Miesian in the regularity and delicacy of its outer shell, eleven-foot cantilevers carrying the metal chassis of the windows well forward of the four ferro-concrete piers.

Large-scale activity in Venezuela is so new and the professional backgrounds of its architects are so various — Villanueva's Paris Ecole des Beaux Arts (of which no trace appears in his current work), Vegas's Illinois Institute of Technology, Benacerraf's Yale, Guinand's and Sanabria's Harvard, Galia's Montevideo, etc. — that it is not so easy as in Brazil, Colombia or Mexico to characterize the new architecture nationally. Large-scale activity predominates in public housing and at the center of the city; apartments are still a relative novelty; and despite the profusion of new houses, modern design for them still seems rather unacclimated and uncertain of its direction. Construction standards are rising rapidly without as yet reaching those of Colombia. The speed of production is striking in a part of the world where, in general, building workers operate with almost medieval deliberation. The energetic urbanism of Maurice Rotival is preparing a frame unique in Latin America for a brand new metropolis of the third quarter of the twentieth century. It will never have the enormous size of Mexico or Buenos Aires nor the relaxed charm of Rio, but with its admirable mountain-backed site and spectacular cloudscapes it already provides a more advanced sketch of the modern city than even São Paulo.

In the more southerly countries of the South American continent architectural production is profuse and in general taste is more conservative. Both statements are least true of Peru, but outside the public housing there is not much notable current work. The University City between Lima and Callao is barely started. However, the school of architecture at the Escuela Nacional de Ingenieros by Bianco is a relatively modest but competent job. The new ministries have an almost Mexican bombast, but the tall buildings that are beginning to rise to the west of the old city along the widened Avenida Taona are quieter in design and not unpleasant in color. As has been said earlier, in the dry climate of Peru painted stucco offers fewer maintenance problems than elsewhere. Despite the local tradition in color, which is rather sober and bichromatic, the new buildings tend to be elaborately colored, but there seems to be no particularly characteristic gamut of tone beyond a general preference for pale prettyish hues. In the very considerable production of new houses south of the city, there are very few of much individual distinction. Some of the new apartment buildings along the Avenida Guzmán Blanco are of better quality, but there are few of these as yet. In general, the old city, as completed in the earlier decades of this century, outweighs in this former vice-regal capital the mid-twentieth century city in interest.

Chile and Uruguay have relatively less new architecture than Peru but the standards of design are higher. As has been said, both countries have excellent architectural schools and now that a change in public taste seems to be taking place, the younger architects should be able to carry on from where older architects like Larrain and Vilamajó left off. Certain Chilean houses and the newest apartment blocks along the beaches in Montevideo compare favorably with the best Latin American work elsewhere.

Curiously enough some of the best Argentine work is to be found in Uruguay, where the holiday resort, Punta Ballena, has a clubhouse and several individual houses by Antonio Bonet, Spanish-born but settled in Buenos Aires. For five years now the Argentines have not been allowed by their government to come to Uruguay, and the houses, unfortunately, are not occupied. There is more activity at the larger nearby resort of Punta del

SCULPTURE BY JEAN ARP SEEN AGAINST
VILLANUEVA'S COVERED PLAZA AND LIBRARY,
UNIVERSITY CITY, CARACAS, VENEZUELA, 1954

STAINED GLASS WINDOWS BY FERNAND LÉGER
IN VILLANUEVA'S LIBRARY, UNIVERSITY CITY,
CARACAS, VENEZUELA, 1954

SCULPTURE BY ANTOINE PEVSNER SEEN AGAINST CARLOS RAÚL VILLANUEVA'S AULA MAGNA WITH MURALS BY
MATTEO MANAURE, UNIVERSITY CITY, CARACAS, VENEZUELA, 1954

MARIO BIANCO: DEPARTMENT OF ARCHITECTURE, NATIONAL SCHOOL FOR ENGINEERS, CAMINO A ANCON, LIMA, PERU, 1952-54

OPPOSITE: CENTER OF CARACAS INCLUDING CENTRO BOLÍVAR, VENEZUELA

GUILLERMO JONES·ODRIOZOLO: HOUSE FOR THE ARCHITECT, PUNTA BALLENA, URUGUAY

OPPOSITE: ANTONIO BONET: CLUBHOUSE, PUNTA BALLENA, URUGUAY, 1947-48

NEW OFFICE BUILDINGS, HAVANA, CUBA

Este where Jones Odriozolo is responsible for the replanning of the area and he and others are building many new houses, his own showing Wrightian influence almost unique in Latin America.

In Argentina there has been little development beyond what has been called the "false dawn" of modern architecture there some ten years ago. But at a town again called La Plata there is the only work by Le Corbusier on this side of the Atlantic. Business buildings and apartment houses in considerable quantity maintain at their best the median level of Latin American work in these fields. The imaginative projects of Amancio Williams that have been widely publicized remain unrealized.

The Curuchet house at La Plata occupies a restricted urban site and it is interesting to see how differently Le Corbusier has handled the three-dimensional composition here. He has lifted the rather restricted living quarters of the house to the third storey above the intermediate floor, where Doctor Curuchet has his office, criss-crossing the space below with ramps. This is opposed to the horizontal development and patio living areas of characteristic Latin American houses. Despite the sharp colonial influence general in these communities, it is evident that only certain aspects of the European architecture have been followed.

In the Caribbean, Havana is a city comparable in size and activity to the capitals on the mainland. Not uncharacteristically, the most striking new edifice here is a nightclub, the nightclub La Tropicana. One would hardly guess that this virtuoso exercise in shell vaulting is by an architect trained at Georgia Institute of Technology and Harvard. Aquiles Capablanca's Tribunal de Cuentas is perhaps the most satisfactory of the many government office buildings of the last few years erected or in the process of being erected in various Latin American capitals. But it is hard to find a common Cuban denominator between its matter-of-factness and the fantasy of La Tropicana. Many new business buildings by other architects reach a higher level of interest than those of Peru or Argentina and extend the range of sun control devices so widely exploited throughout Latin America. Painted stucco is the rule here and colors are often strong and rich, but not aggressive in the Mexican way. By contrast, Harrison and Abramovitz' American Embassy, standing in splendid isolation on the waterfront, has a cool and untropical look. Lacking the usual Latin American devices for sun control, it has the distinction (like the similar but much less successful Embassy in Rio by the same architects) of all-over sheathing with imported travertine. This edifice, perhaps the most satisfactory of a good many throughout Latin America by architects from the States, helps to point up the qualities that differentiate Latin American modern architecture from that of North America, though so many local architects in Colombia and in Venezuela, as well as in Cuba, received their training here.

It is not surprising that this training is even more universal in Puerto Rico, and despite the skillful adaptation to a near tropical climate, the Caribe Hilton Hotel, by Toro, Ferrer and Torregrossa, appears very North American (the interiors, in fact, were carried out by the New York firm of Warner-Leeds). Thus far it seems to be the most successful of the resort hotels in Latin America. Although in effect merely another state university like those in the States, the plans of the President of the University of Puerto Rico, Jaime Benitez, for future construction there, are almost comparable in extent to the University Cities of other Latin American countries. Henry Klumb has already executed four or five buildings at the university and considerable faculty housing. But his most interesting work is a church, the Blessed Martín de Porres, at Bayview, Cataño, near San Juan. This is exceptional not only in its highly original handling of the unglazed openings in the walls but, since Niemeyer's and de la Mora's churches of a decade ago, in being about the only ecclesiastical modern structure of any quality built in Latin America.

In this Commonwealth, this free associated state,* where Latin America and the United States overlap, it is not inappropriate that Klumb, the only Wright disciple in all Latin America, should be working with real success to adopt the principles of the Master of Taliesin to the material conditions of the Caribbean. But as the economy of this Commonwealth expands, local architects trained in the States should also have much to contribute, as the nearly completed airport and the Supreme Court building by Toro-Ferrer indicate perhaps better than their hotel. Already certain of their houses, such as that for Teodoro Moscoso, the head of the Industrial Development Corporation, have a special quality in the planning which effectively combines North American and Latin American ideas.

But it is naturally not in Puerto Rico that one finds the most intense expression of Latin American potentialities in architecture. Before turning to the

* Estado Libro Asociado is the Spanish designation of the Commonwealth of Puerto Rico.

HENRY KLUMB: LIBRARY, UNIVERSITY OF PUERTO RICO, RIO PIEDRAS

TORO-FERRER: HOUSE FOR
TEODORO MOSCOSO, SANTURCE,
PUERTO RICO, 1950

RINO LEVI AND ROBERTO CERQUEIRA
CESAR: MILTON GUPER HOUSE,
RUA NICARAGUA 254, JARDIM
AMERICA, SÃO PAULO, BRAZIL,
1951-53

discussion of individual industrial buildings, it may be well to make a few concluding general statements about modern architecture in Latin America. It still belongs, if not to the "International Style," a concept now somewhat too narrow for modern architecture as it has developed in the last thirty years, to the general international current that has flowed ever more strongly and broadly since the 1920s. Its local idioms relate most closely, as is natural, to those of the Latin countries of southern Europe. Of the great international masters, the influence of Le Corbusier is strongest and appropriately he is the one great architect of the outside world who has not only acted as a consultant on a major monument — the Ministry of Education and Public Health in Rio — but has actually built in Latin America.

The characteristic structural material is ferro-concrete, chiefly in conventional cage construction, but sometimes in thin shell forms. Color, generally paint over stucco but increasingly mosaic of glass, or tile, is more widely used than anywhere else in the world, and on the whole perhaps more successfully. Two-dimensional art, panels of *azulejos* or figural mosaic, is much employed, often with real distinction. The climate generally demands sun control and this is provided by many different devices all of which provide very characteristic plastic effects or façades. Public monuments are more significant than private houses; business blocks and public housing more successful than apartment blocks. Except in the work of Niemeyer, intensely personal expression is rare; but so young are most of the active practitioners — some still in their twenties — that other individual talents of real consequence may well be maturing. The general tendency is to plan big and build slow, but there are notable exceptions — where else but in Venezuela could a housing development of the scale of Cerro Piloto be begun and finished inside of a year? Maintenance is generally poor, but the problem of so surfacing buildings that they will long remain both physically and visually in good condition preoccupies many architects. Houses of distinctively local character are found chiefly in Mexico and Brazil; elsewhere the achievement of viable modern house planning for local needs probably lies a few years ahead. Apartment houses are spreading rapidly to cities that have never previously known them. Good churches are disappointingly few.

Finally: modern architecture in Latin America has its own intrinsic values which the following collection of individual findings attempts to make evident by a rigid selection of examples. Quite obviously, because of its many common problems, knowledge of the architecture of one Latin American country can and should be of great value to the others. Despite the lack of a single cultural metropolis, either in the Latin homelands of Europe or in the New World, further development should be on a common front. Niemeyer has had a great influence in the other countries. Brazil in return might profitably learn something of sounder building techniques from Colombia or Venezuela. But just as the exhibition "Brazil Builds" a dozen years ago not only signalled the appearance of a vigorous new local school of modern architecture, the Cariocan, but caused some of the innovations of that school to enter the common language of the outside world, so Latin American architecture, apprehended as a whole, may well have something more than a few clichés of *brise-soleils*, shell vaults and *azulejos* to offer the rest of the world. Partly, modern architecture has grown by following leaders — Le Corbusier, Gropius, Mies, Frank Lloyd Wright — but also it has always grown on broader fronts. For good or for ill, it is international in its future. Everywhere there can be profit from the exchange of ideas. In modern architecture North America has given much and received much. To Latin America it has already given a great deal and will doubtless give much more. But there is much also that we can profitably receive, particularly now that Western European production is so low in quantity and so inhibited by economic difficulties. In architecture Latin America is more than able to hold its own with the rest of the Western World. It is not inappropriate that the principal international awards in architecture are now those given at the São Paulo Biennal.

Late comer though Latin America has been in the world of modern architecture, there are many reasons why it should flourish there as well as other reasons why it developed an autochthonous character. An expanding economy required many new types of structures for which there was neither local nor academic precedent. With the fading prestige of the Paris Ecole des Beaux Arts, architects turned to more active centers of contemporary building for inspiration; or more precisely to those established new traditions of modern design which have increasingly replaced the so-called "traditional" in Western Europe and America during the past thirty years.

But local problems needed local solutions and the exchange of ideas gave to these local solutions, at first largely Cariocan, a broader base in the experience of several countries.

Considered as a whole and measured against the achievement of Western Europe or of North America in the first half of the twentieth century, the achievement of Latin America up to the present lacks work by leaders such as Le Corbusier or Wright; but if the comparison be limited to the post-war years during which production in Europe has been very restricted and few new leaders of distinction have appeared, Latin America excels both in quantity and quality. It is less easy to compare Latin American architecture with post-war architecture of the United States, but the selections of buildings in this book and in *Built in U. S. A.* allow some conclusions. The forty-six Latin American buildings, even if they include no Johnson Wax tower and no Lake Shore Drive apartments, considered as a group certainly rival in general interest the forty-three buildings in the North American volume. At least ten architects in the Latin American group have produced work of such distinguished individual quality that their names deserve to be as well-known as those of their contemporaries in the States.

To the roster of great modern buildings Latin America has added a fair quota; to the pool of accomplished contemporary construction it has added proportionately more. It would not have been difficult to add another twenty-five buildings of quality equal to those selected; had projects and buildings already partly completed been considered for inclusion, the number would have easily been doubled. But the forty-six buildings that follow should prove that modern architecture in Latin America has indeed, in this decade, come of age.

PLATES

1 NIEMEYER

IGREJA DE SÃO FRANCISCO, PAMPULHA, BRAZIL

1 Oscar NIEMEYER Soares Filho

IGREJA DE SÃO FRANCISCO (CHURCH OF ST. FRANCIS)
PAMPULHA, NEAR BELO HORIZONTE, MINAS GERAIS, BRAZIL.
1943
JOAQUIM CARDOZO, STRUCTURAL ENGINEER

In this church Niemeyer continued the brilliant promise of his
work of the previous five years. The free curves characteristic
of his planning are here disciplined into the structural curves
of the paraboloid shell vaults. The conoidal section of the
nave vault allows brilliant light to fall on the altar—had one
been installed—and on the frescoed east wall by Cândido
Portinari. Less happy, particularly at this chapel-like scale,
is the rather freehand use of curves and diagonals in the belfry
and entrance shelter. Louvers temper the western light in the
upper portion of the front. The mural on the outside of the
east wall, executed in *azulejos* (painted tiles) is Portinari's
finest work of this typically Brazilian order. Characteristic is
the background of wallpaper-like repeated motifs, and effectively complementary to the relatively simple structural curves
of the sanctuary and sacristy are the strong free curves linking
the figures in the composition. As the bishop refused to
consecrate the church it has never been used for its intended
purposes; but it is (very properly despite its extreme youth)
now under the protection of SPHAN (Serviço do Pâtrimonio
Histórico e Artístico Nacional).

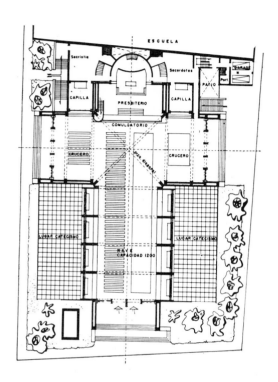

2 Enrique DE LA MORA y Palomar
IGLESIA DE LA PURÍSIMA (CHURCH OF LA PURÍSIMA)
MONTERREY, MEXICO, 1947

Originally designed even earlier than Niemeyer's São Francisco, this church, with its cruciform plan and apse, is considerably more conventional and much less effectively lighted. The ribs, and above all the purlin-like horizontal member in the interior, diminish the effectiveness of the paraboloid vault. Sculpture, rather than murals, provides the figural embellishment. Since the interior photograph was taken, stained glass has been introduced with a none too happy effect. Despite all these minor qualifications this remains one of the most successful of twentieth-century Catholic churches and has been influential abroad.

69

3 Henry KLUMB

IGLESIA DEL BEATO MARTÍN DE PORRES
(CHURCH OF THE BLESSED MARTÍN PORRES)
BAYVIEW, CATANO, NEAR SAN JUAN, PUERTO RICO. 1950

Entirely different from Niemeyer's and de la Mora's vaulted churches, and lacking their dramatic spatial effects, this edifice handles tropical problems of ventilation and controlled lighting with great success. The upper portions of the walls are unglazed, being mere screens of timber-like concrete members over which vines hang to temper the light. The diagonally placed piers provide further light baffles. Wide-angle photographs unfortunately distort the interior spatial effect which is more firmly directed on the crucifix by Father Marcolino Maas than the photograph shows. More conventional in plan than Wright's churches, it lacks their vigorous external expression but has an appropriately devotional feeling inside, such as they generally lack.

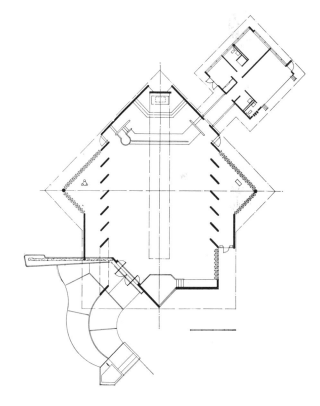

4 Aquiles CAPABLANCA Y GRAUPERA
TRIBUNAL DE CUENTAS (OFFICE OF THE COMPTROLLER)
CARRETERA DE RANCHOS BOYERES, HAVANA, CUBA. 1952-54

This building, housing certain financial departments of the Cuban government in a new administrative city outside the old town on the way to the airport, is one of the least grandiose and visually aggressive of the many government buildings lately risen or still rising in Latin American capitals. Following in general the Corbusian formula introduced at the Ministry of Education in Rio fifteen years earlier, it has a certain masculinity of detailing which is more Gropius-like. Especially effective both in its warm beige tone and its rough texture is the limestone, with coarse shell aggregate, with which the walls are sheathed. The large bronze statue, inferior intrinsically to Lipchitz's *Prometheus* on the Rio Ministry of Education but better scaled, and the bold mosaic by Amelia Pelaez, are characteristic of the Latin American use of other arts to elaborate and give interest even to buildings predominantly utilitarian in character.

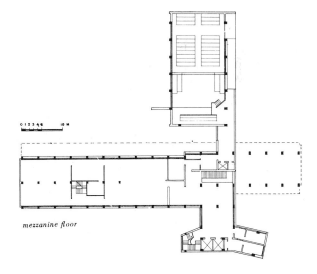

mezzanine floor

73

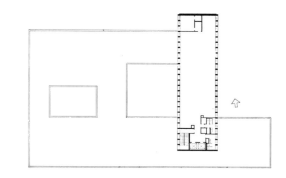

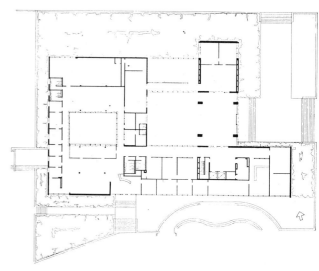

Perhaps more typical of Italy than of North America, this official U.S. Government building by a leading New York firm
points up some of the special local characteristics of Latin
American modern architecture by its contrast with Capablanca's Tribunal de Cuentas. No sculpture or mosaics are
used here and the travertine surfacing, handsome though it is,
lacks the local savor of the figured limestone on the Tribunal.
Only the low block at the base provides architectural sun control — glare is taken care of by green-tinted glass — and the
general understatement in the plastic organization of the
blocks and in the handling of the surfaces contrasts with the
bold effects usual with Latin Americans.

5 HARRISON and ABRAMOVITZ

AMERICAN EMBASSY
MALECÓN AT CALLE CALZADA, HAVANA, CUBA. 1952-53

6 Juan O'GORMAN, Gustavo SAAVEDRA, and Juan MARTÍNEZ DE VELASCO
BIBLIOTECA CENTRAL (CENTRAL LIBRARY). CIUDAD UNIVERSITARIA, MEXICO, D.F. 1951-53

Although neither the largest nor the loudest of the buildings of the Mexican University City, the library is certainly the most original. Painter today more than architect, although he was one of the first to introduce modern architecture to Mexico twenty years ago, O'Gorman has used the blank walls of his stack-tower, unbroken except for tiny stair windows, like the pages of an illustrated codex. The colors of the mosaic, executed with rough lumps of natural minerals rather than with glass tesserae, are remarkably soft and rich, while the scale and texture is definitely architectural. Architectural also is the lava wall below with its bold relief. Unfortunately, the more conventional portions of the structure are rather awkwardly detailed and the colors of the Mexican onyx used to temper the light in the upper sash of the reading rooms, not to speak of the red-painted metalwork, accord ill with tones of the mosaic. Although the enormous Ministry of Communications and Public Works of Carlos Lazo has since outbid the library in the extent and the aggressiveness of its mosaic-covered walls, this remains the most successful example of the large-scale use of figural decoration in modern architecture, to . which the Mexicans are especially addicted.

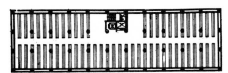

typical stack floor

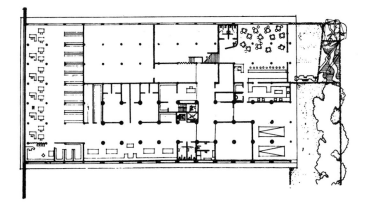

7 Carlos Raúl VILLANUEVA

AULA MAGNA AND PLAZA CUBIERTA
(AUDITORIUM AND COVERED PLAZA)
CIUDAD UNIVERSITARIA, CARACAS, VENEZUELA. 1952-53

The auditorium, with the related foyers, covered but only partially enclosed, of the University at Caracas, among a large group of edifices already completed there or still in construction, rival the buildings of the Mexican University City in boldness and in the profuse use of associated works of art. Inside the auditorium the remarkable ceiling, worked out by the architect in association with the acoustic specialist Robert Newman and the sculptor Alexander Calder, is certainly one of the most striking examples in the world, both by its scale and by its architectural integration, of a collaborative project. Externally the auditorium from the rear and sides is rather stern and masculine, its concrete skeleton completely exposed below the tremendous proscenium truss and its panels filled with grey glass mosaic. Much more ingratiating is the extensive Plaza Cubierta — almost a "covered campus" rather than merely the foyer of the auditorium, with grove-like ranges of light concrete columns, and prefabricated grills through which the tremendously strong light of Caracas filters delicately; sculptures by Arp and others as well as free-standing mosaic screens by Léger and various Venezuelans, produce a sort of contemporary museum half in- and half out-of-doors.

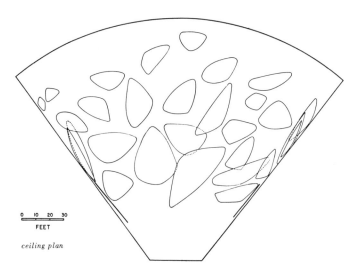

0 10 20 30
FEET

ceiling plan

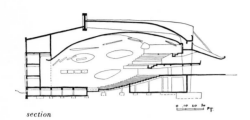

section

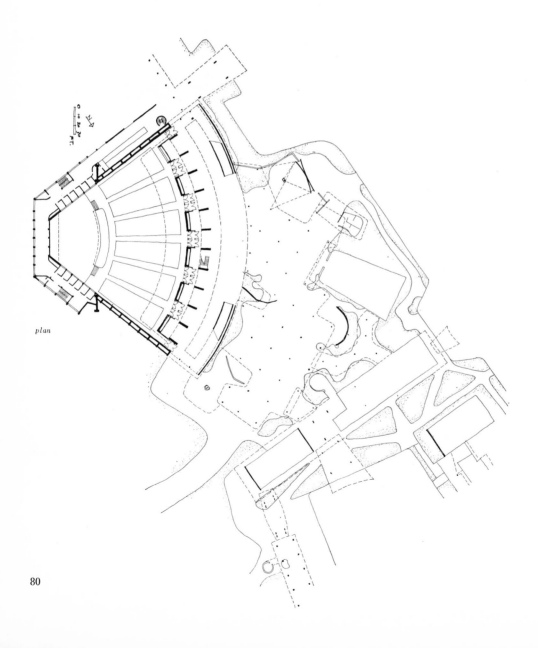

plan

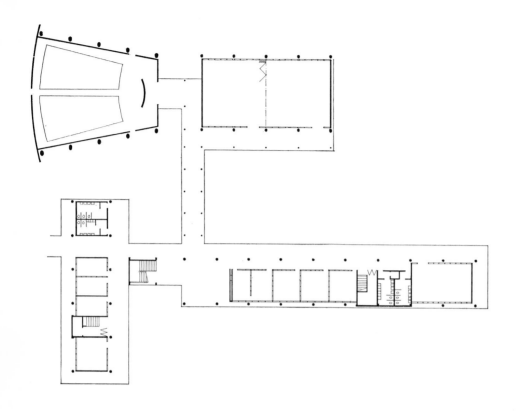

The University City of Panama naturally does not rival in size or complexity those of larger countries like Mexico and Venezuela. The group of related buildings housing the School of Public Administration and business lacks the assertiveness of O'Gorman's or Villanueva's work. The natural mahogany louvers, the carefully selected plain brown tiles in two tones, and the boldly colored and patterned tiles imported from Valencia in Spain provide considerable interest in detail, even though some of the more striking formal elements are patently borrowed from the Cariocan School.

8 Guillermo DE ROUX, René BRENES, and Ricardo BERMÚDEZ
ESCUELA DE ADMINISTRACIÓN Y COMERCIO (SCHOOL OF ADMINISTRATION AND BUSINESS)
UNIVERSIDAD DE PANAMÁ, PANAMA, REPUBLIC OF PANAMA. 1949-53

9 Jorge Machado MOREIRA
INSTITUTO DE PUERICULTURA (CHILDREN'S CLINIC)
CIDADE UNIVERSITARIA, RIO DE JANEIRO, BRAZIL. 1953

This small but complex building housing a children's clinic and a nursery school, associated with the Polyclinic Hospital rising nearby, is the only completed structure at the Rio University City. Extremely quiet in design, it has much refinement in detail and is executed with a care unusual in Rio. Many of the characteristic elements of Brazilian modern architecture are to be seen here, *azulejos* by Burle-Marx, open screens made up of tile elements, roof shelters of shell-vaulting, but all handled with the utmost restraint.

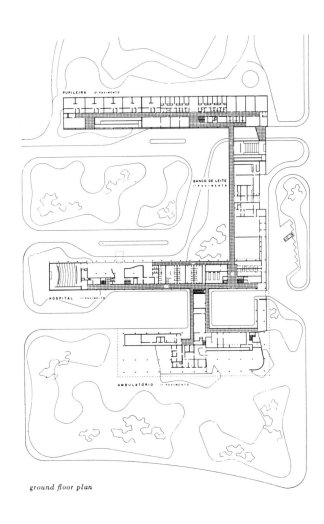

ground floor plan

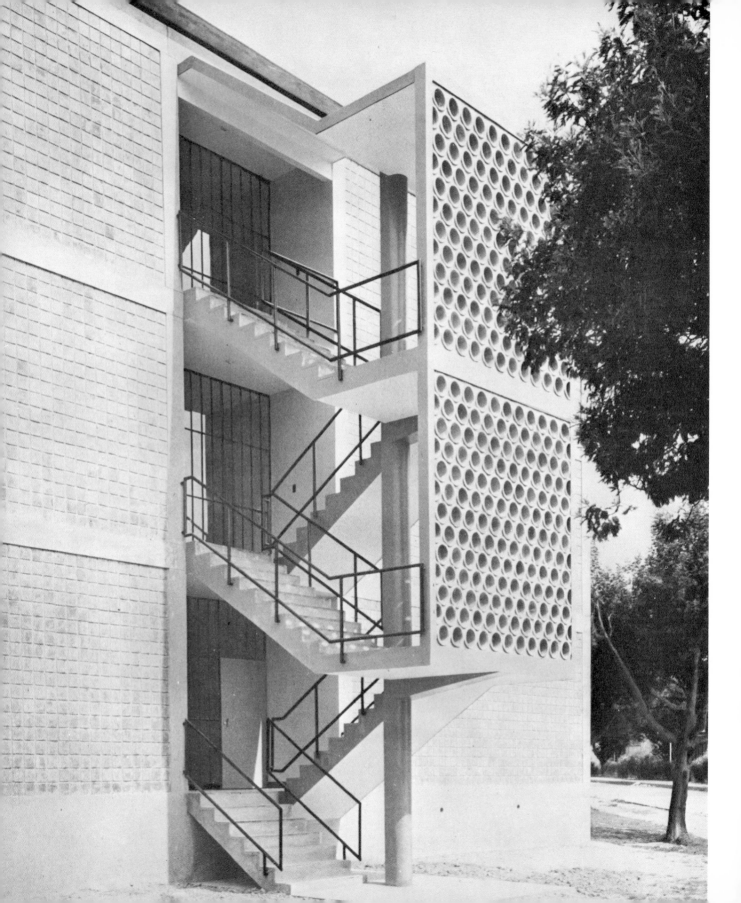

10 CUELLAR, SERRANO, GÓMEZ y Cia, Ltda
CURSO PREPARATORIO (PREPARATORY SCHOOL)
CIUDAD UNIVERSITARIA, BOGOTÁ, COLOMBIA. 1951-52

This university classroom edifice well illustrates the directness
and competence of Colombian building. With no panoply of
mosaics or *azulejos*, Serrano has used an almost industrial vocabulary of exposed concrete skeleton with tile infilling to
excellent, if quite unmonumental, effect. Unfortunately the
University City of Bogotá has no over-all architectural discipline and the campus exhibits all the variety of an American
University. None of the other new buildings, except the unfinished chapel and the Centro Interamericano de Vivienda
(Inter-American Housing Center) are comparable in quiet
excellence to this.

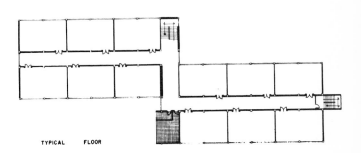

TYPICAL   FLOOR

section

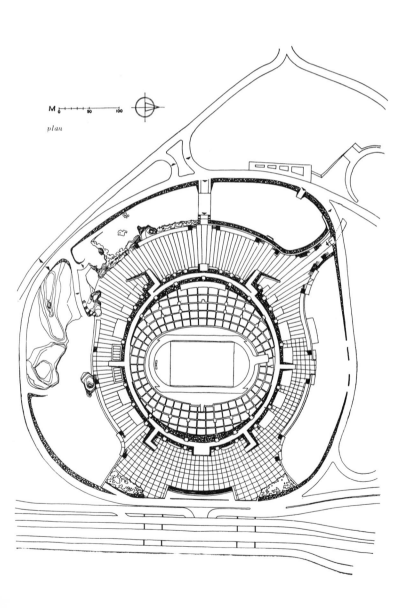

M |⊢⊢⊢⊢⊢⊢⊢⊢| 50 | 100   ⊕

plan

11 Augusto PÉREZ PALACIOS, Raúl SALINAS Moro, and Jorge BRAVO Jiménez
ESTADIO OLÍMPICO (OLYMPIC STADIUM)
CIUDAD UNIVERSITARIA, MEXICO, D.F. 1951-52

Created by scooping out the earth from the center and piling it up to form the stands this stadium, faced with concrete and lava blocks, has an almost prehistoric scale without in any way imitating prehistoric architectural forms. The long sweep of the upper edge, an ellipse moving in three dimensions over and around the circle of the playing field, above sloping banks broken by boldly scaled portals, successfully combines lyric elegance with massive monumentality. Like O'Gorman, Diego Rivera used various colored minerals for the figural decoration on the front, a composition in whose elements Indian feeling is very strong. But the vigorous relief of the design and the ingenious exploitation of various textures is admirably related to the plain lava walling in which it is set.

12 Carlos Raúl VILLANUEVA
ESTADIO OLÍMPICO (OLYMPIC STADIUM)
CIUDAD UNIVERSITARIA, CARACAS, VENEZUELA. 1950-51

Characteristically Latin American is this stadium at the University City of Caracas, with its grandstand covered by a boldly cantilevered shell concrete marquee. Mosaic both plain and figural is used, but only quite incidentally. As with Villanueva's other work at the University, his handling of the exposed concrete is extremely bold, but the curves of the shell vault are not without their lyric grace.

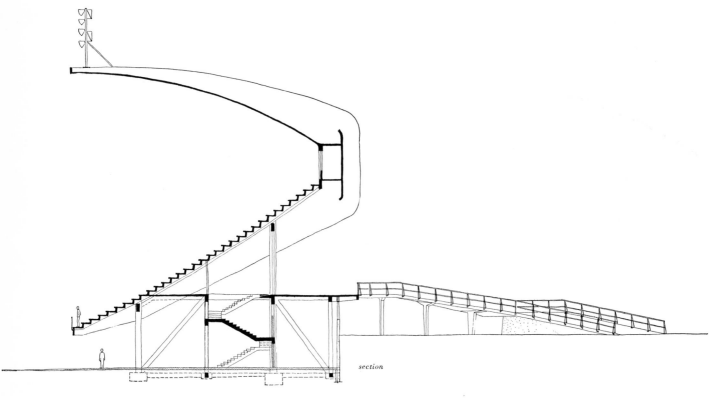

section

12 VILLANUEVA
ESTADIO OLÍMPICO, CARACAS, VENEZUELA

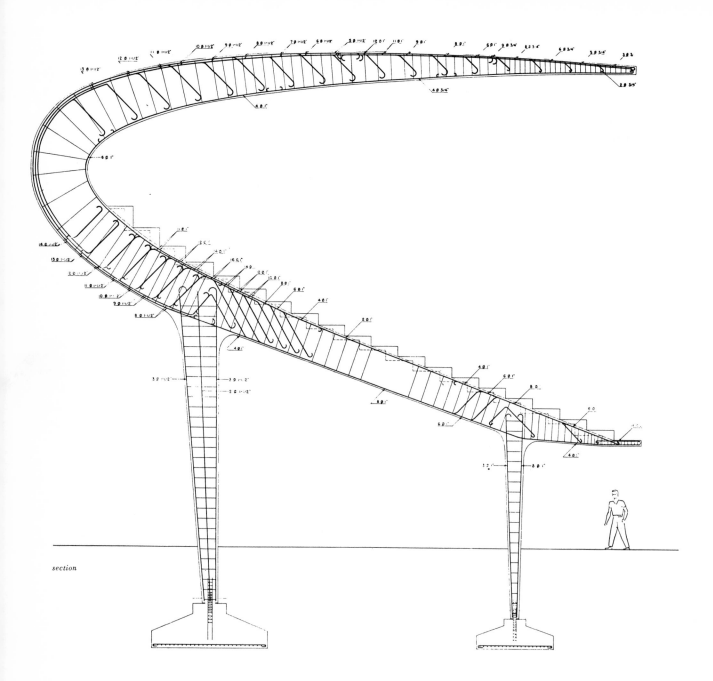

section

98

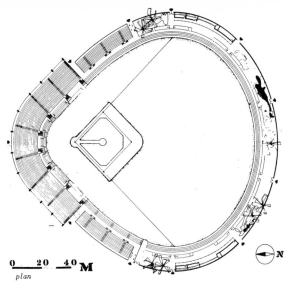

0 20 40 **M**
plan

13 Mesa Gabriel SOLANO, Jorge GAITÁN Cortés, Alvaro ORTEGA, and Edgar BURBANO; Guillermo GONZÁLEZ Zuleta, engineer
ESTADIO DE BASE-BALL (BASEBALL STADIUM) CARTAGENA, COLOMBIA. 1947

Larger and lighter than the Caracas stadium, this is one of the most striking examples in the world of cantilevered shell vaulting. The vigorous curvature of the plan and the recurrent openings at the rear of the stands as well as the remarkably clean continuity of line in the ribs provide an almost awning-like effect of tenuity unequalled in any similar construction.

14 Icaro de Castro MELLO

PISCINA DO DEPARTAMENTO DE ESPORTES
DO ESTADO DE SÃO PAULO
(POOL, DEPARTMENT OF SPORTS OF THE STATE OF SÃO PAULO)
RUA DA. GERMAINE BURCHARD 451,
SÃO PAULO, BRAZIL. 1952-53

Elegant in its engineering conception, if rather clumsily detailed architecturally, the aluminum sheathed shell vault covering this swimming pool is one of the largest of its type in the world. Here the ubiquitous curves of Brazilian modern architecture, too frequently rather petty, have, as in Niemeyer's church, structural justification and splendid scale.

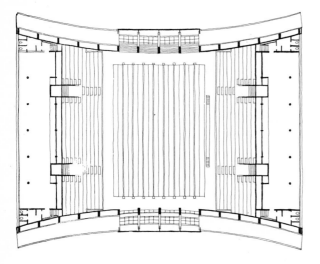

15 Mesa Gabriel SOLANO and Alvaro ORTEGA;
Guillermo GONZÁLEZ Zuleta, engineer

TALLER Y ESTACIÓN DE BUSES (WORKSHOP AND BUS STATION)
CALLE 68 AT CARRERA 46, BOGOTÁ, COLOMBIA. 1947

In these bus repair shops tile-reinforced shell vaults are used
in the most direct and utilitarian fashion with walls of plain
brick.

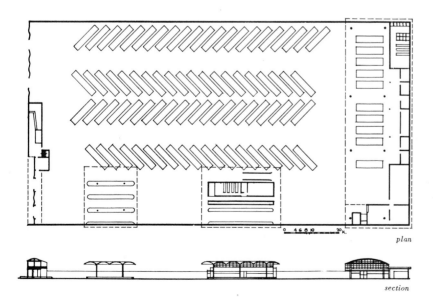

plan

section

16 Alejandro PRIETO; Félix CANDELA, contracting engineer

LABORATORIES CIBA (CIBA LABORATORIES)
CALZADA DE TLALPAN AT 20 DE AGOSTO, MEXICO, D.F.
1953-54

This pharmaceutical plant designed for a Swiss firm has many Mexican characteristics. The large mural in mosaic rivals in pretension those of the University City, and colored materials are used throughout. The shell vaults of Candela appear in various forms, most strikingly in the large "umbrella" over the porter's lodge and the line of smaller ones leading back from the front office block to the industrial elements at the rear. Although this is a relatively modest example of Candela's engineering in concrete, his cooperation here with the architect has introduced his striking forms in a total complex of architectural rather than engineering character.

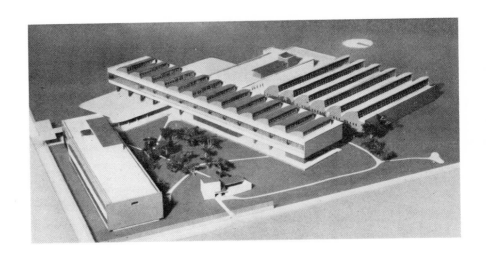

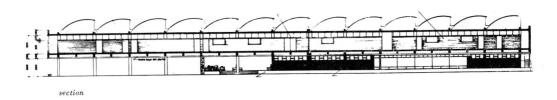

section

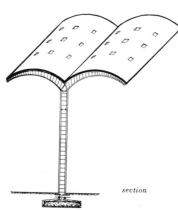

section

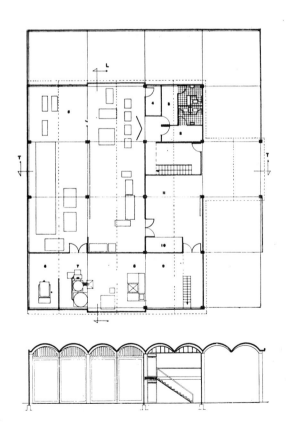

17 Francisco PIZANO
FÁBRICA DE CHICLES CLARK'S (CLARK'S CHICLE FACTORY)
CALLE 19A AT CARRERA 34, BOGOTÁ, COLOMBIA. 1953

In this chewing gum factory the prefabricated shell vault elements of Solano y Ortega are skillfully utilized. The finish of the concrete elements reflects the Colombian work of Violi, a Perret pupil, and well illustrates the high quality of structural technique in Bogotá. Latin American factories are generally very small by North American standards, but several in Colombia have architectonic qualities rare in the States and indicate that Latin American architects often give to such work, with its opportunities for technical innovations, their best thought.

18 Max BORGES, Jr.

CABARET TROPICANA
AVENIDA TRUFFIN, HAVANA, CUBA. 1952

This Cuban night club exhibits a far more melodramatic use
of shell-vaulting than the industrial buildings of Mexico and
Colombia, almost rivaling in scale the Latin American stadiums. But the elements here, set down under great trees
which here and there cut through them, are exploited for their
lyricism and for the curious cave-like but not oppressive spatial
effects they can produce. Shelter is here etherealized not by
reduction of supporting and supported members but by the
almost freehand fashion in which the successive curved planes
of the shells are related in space. The result rivals in autochthonous Latin American quality the work of Niemeyer.

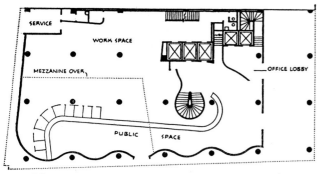

ground floor

19 Oscar NIEMEYER Soares Filho
BANCO BOAVISTA (BOAVISTA BANK)
PRAÇA PIO X, 118, RIO DE JANEIRO, BRAZIL. 1946

In this banking house Niemeyer has varied his sun control devices according to orientation, yet kept a consistent scale and
degree of plastic interest throughout. The sinuous curve of the
ground storey screen-wall of glass brick, winding in and out
between the columns, well expresses its non-structural character. Unlike so many business structures in Rio, this building is well maintained, largely because the surfacing materials
were carefully chosen and well put together. Built relatively
early, the bank set a pace for Latin American business buildings that has not always been successfully kept up even by
Niemeyer himself.

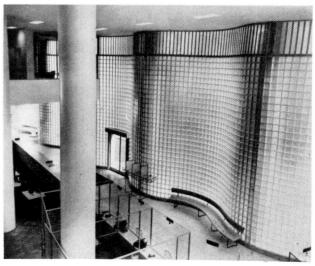

20 Ricardo DE ROBINA and
Jaime ORTIZ MONASTERIO

EDIFICIO VALENZUELA (OFFICE BUILDING)
67 CALLE DE NIZA, MEXICO, D.F.

This is exceptional among glassfronted buildings for the clarity of its design, the size of its sheets of glass, and the excellence of its proportions; the usual flatness is avoided by the introduction of projecting concrete elements. The organization of these within the firm frame of concrete at the sides and top provides an abstract design of real subtlety. This is nonetheless truly architectural and not merely an imitation of a Neo-Plasticist painting.

21 Martín VEGAS Pacheco y José Miguel GALIA

EDIFICIO POLAR (POLAR BUILDING)
PLAZA VENEZUELA, CARACAS, VENEZUELA. 1952-54

Rivaling in height the undistinguished Centro Bolívar, the "Rockefeller Center" of downtown Caracas, this isolated uptown skyscraper is little related to other Latin American work. The structure is ferro-concrete, but eleven-foot cantilevers on all four sides carry the steel chassis well forward of the four piers that sustain the building. In this chassis, glass, solid-louvered sash, and sandwich panels (plywood inside and aluminum outside) are combined in different proportions on the four sides according to the incidence of the powerful Caracas sunshine. Vegas' training under Mies at Illinois Institute of Technology is evident in the care with which the over-all pattern of the sash has been handled. Color is very discreet, indeed merely incidental. The lightness of the general effect is most striking, as is also the isolated location of this tower rising above such one-storey structures as Don Hatch's Chrysler salesroom on the right. Here one sees how the carefully planned expansion of Caracas is producing a new city of the mid-twentieth century and not merely filling up a colonial town with tall new structures, as is the case in most other Latin American capitals.

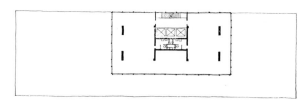

typical floor

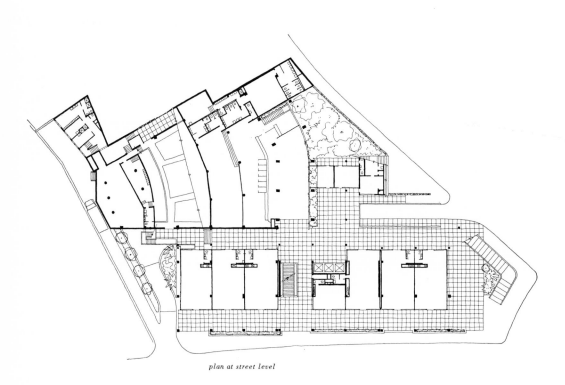

plan at street level

21 VEGAS and GALIA
EDIFICIO POLAR, CARACAS, VENEZUELA

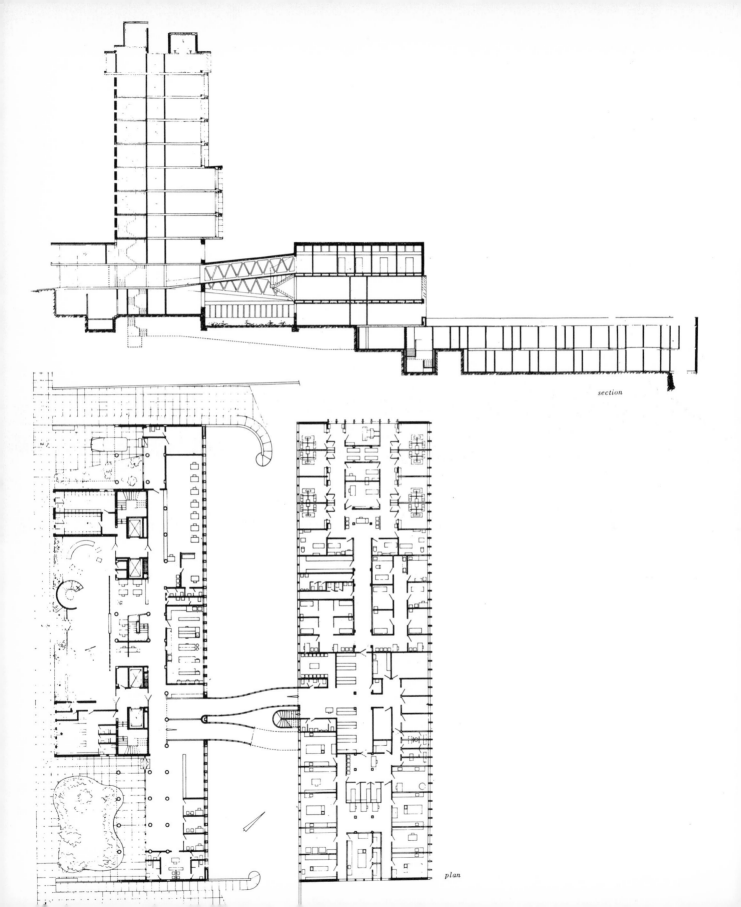

section

plan

22 Rino LEVI and Roberto Cerqueira CESAR
INSTITUTO CENTRAL DO CANCER
(CANCER HOSPITAL AND CLINIC)
RUA JOSÉ GETULIO, SÃO PAULO, BRAZIL. 1949-54

This cancer clinic and hospital in São Paulo is an impressively large and straightforward edifice, skillfully organized — particularly as regards the handling of the section — in two parallel blocks on a hillside site. Naturally lacking the virtuoso flourishes of Cariocan architecture, this nevertheless makes the most of its difficult but dramatic site, building up handsomely from the garden court on which certain public rooms open at the rear.

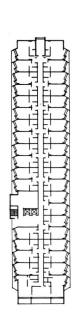

typical floor

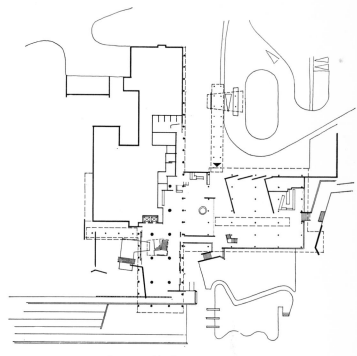

plan at ground level

23 TORO, FERRER y TORREGROSSA;
Warner-Leeds, interiors

CARIBE HILTON HOTEL
SAN JUAN, PUERTO RICO. 1947-49

Running east to west on a fine site by the waterfront, the hotel block consists of bed-sitting-room units each with its own balcony. The canting of the window walls of these units assures privacy to the triangular balconies and improves the view. Like most new hotels in the tropics, this is a complete resort in itself, with a large swimming pool, protected from the ocean by a range of cabanas, various bars, restaurants and even a gaming room. Understandably, Puerto Rican architecture has a more North American flavor than that of other Latin American areas. But the local architects, trained in the States, have utilized their knowledge of the climate and their feeling for the scenery to excellent effect, while turning to a New York firm for the detailed designing and furnishing of the interiors.

24 Mario PANI

CENTRO URBANO PRESIDENTE JUÁREZ
(PRESIDENT JUÁREZ URBAN HOUSING DEVELOPMENT)
AVENIDA ANTONIO ANZA, MEXICO, D.F. 1950-52

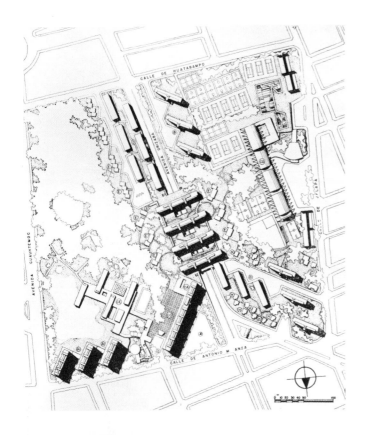

This very extensive housing project for government employees has the advantage of a site relatively near the center of the city yet contiguous to a large tree-shaded park. The wide distribution of the blocks and the skillful combination of edifices of different heights provide a general effect of openness and great variety in the vistas. Some clichés of Cariocan origin appear in the designing but the general effect is notably Mexican. Toward this the work of the painter Carlos Mérida, who collaborated with the architect, contributes notably. The colored concrete panels are better scaled to the exposed concrete structural elements and brown brick in filling than most Mexican external murals executed in mosaic. Still more effective are the plain-colored balcony parapets on certain of the tall blocks, the strong colors being well chosen to go with the brown brick and organized into an over-all pattern which is neither too regular nor too random. The very positive architectural interest achieved in this project — paralleled to a considerable extent in Pani's other major housing scheme, the Centro Urbano Presidente Alemán — indicates well how high are Latin American ambitions in the field of public building. Unfortunately the quality of the execution is not always up to the quality of the design.

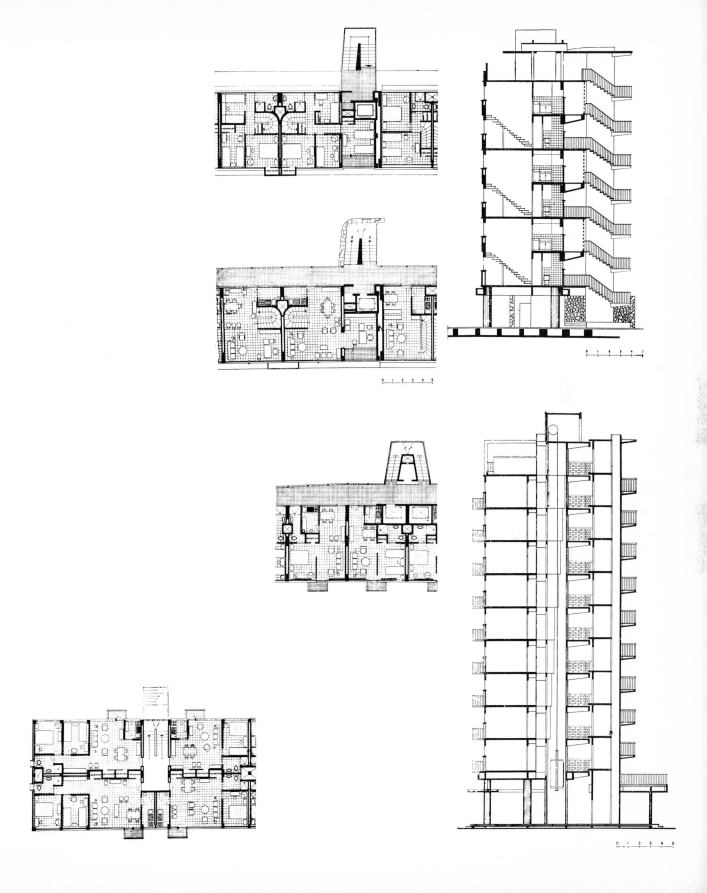

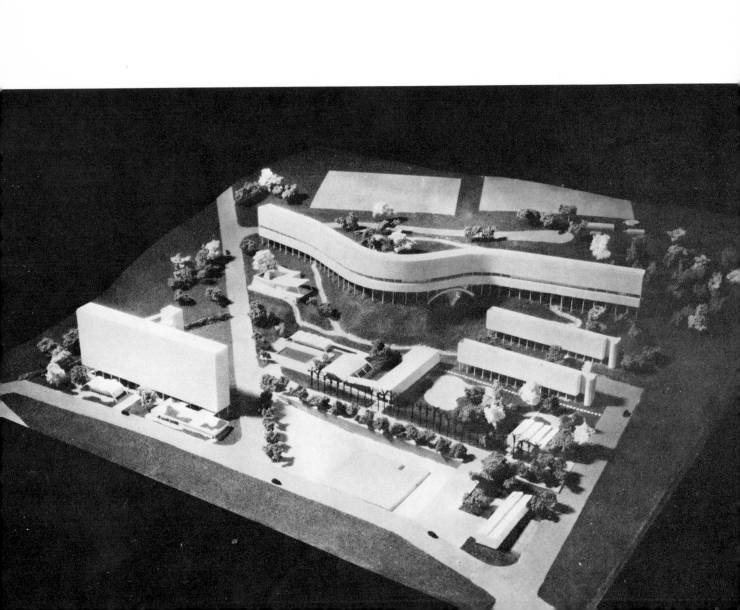

25 Affonso Eduardo REIDY
CONJUNTOS DE APARTAMENTOS
(APARTMENT HOUSING) RUA CAPITÃO FÉLIX,
PEDREGULHO, RIO DE JANEIRO, BRAZIL. 1948-50

Although the long sinuous block high on the hill, recalling certain of Le Corbusier's North African projects, is still unfinished, enough of the Pedregulho project is complete to make it a notable example of twentieth century low-cost housing. Community buildings and a school provide necessary facilities for the inhabitants and also vary the general layout. The rising terrain, with the highest block at the rear half way up the hill, allows the whole scheme to display itself in actuality almost as clearly as in the model. Tile grill work and other sun control devices give a delicacy of scale to the completed housing blocks, and the light colors of the painted stucco are happily accented by panels of *azulejos* on some of the lower structures. When complete the big block, approached by bridges from the hill slope to an entrance floor midway up the building, will be one of the most successful of tall and extended low-cost housing devices.

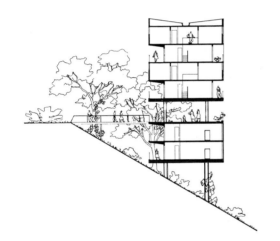

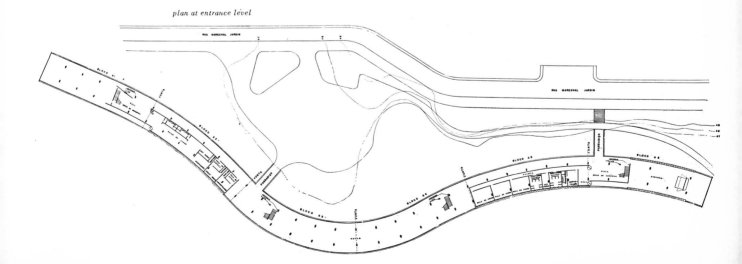

plan at entrance level

25 REIDY

CONJUNTOS DE APARTAMENTOS, RIO DE JANEIRO, BRAZIL

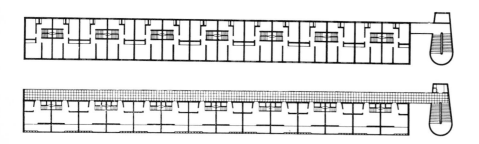

26 Affonso Eduardo REIDY

**ESCOLA PRIMARIA AND GIMNASIO (PRIMARY SCHOOL AND GYMNASIUM)
RUA CAPITÃO FÉLIX, PEDREGULHO, RIO DE JANEIRO, BRAZIL. 1948-50**

In contrast to the rectangular patterns of the executed housing
blocks, the primary school and its associated gymnasium utilize
with brilliance various of the forms which Reidy and his asso-
ciates working under Costa on the Ministry of Education
evolved a decade earlier. The classroom block, raised off the
ground and with a sloping façade to the south, has a corridor
protected from the northern sun by a tile grill. A sloping slab
over an open ramp links the school block with the gymnasium
which is roofed with a low shell vault. Protected by this curv-
ing shell is one of Cândido Portinari's most successful *azulejos*
murals. A tiny wallpaper-like repeating motif of leaping
children is played against the curvilinear sweep of the main
composition. In this group of related structures the special
Cariocan qualities of grace and lightness are as individually
expressed as in anything of Niemeyer's.

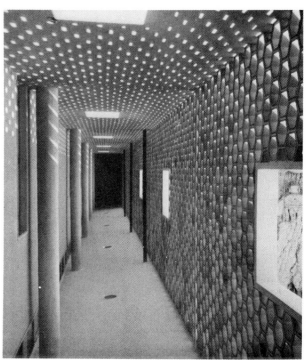

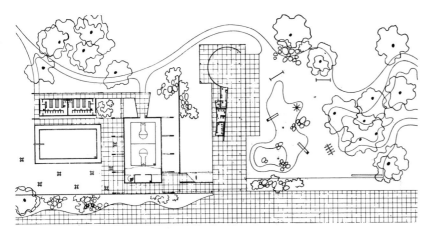

plan at ground level

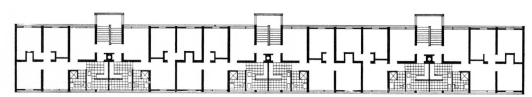

typical floor

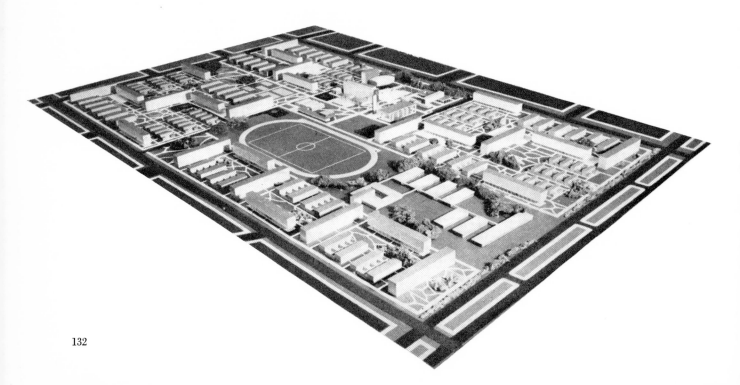

132

27 Santiago AGURTO Calvo

UNIDAD VECINAL MATUTE (MATUTE HOUSING DEVELOPMENT)
LIMA, PERU. 1952

Perhaps the best of the extensive housing developments under-
taken by the Corporación Nacional de la Vivienda (National
Housing Corporation) around Lima is that at Matute, even
though only about two-thirds of the scheme is so far complete.
The open layout with moderately tall walk-up blocks alternating with groups of one-storey houses is orderly and yet pleas-
antly varied. The rendered concrete surfaces are painted in
characteristically Peruvian colors, light and gay under the
white-grey skies and against the muddy-grey mountains. Without the somewhat aggressive monumentality of Pani's Mexican
housing projects or the lyric delicacy of Reidy's work at Pedregulho, Agurto's competent and straightforward housing is
about the best new architecture in Peru.

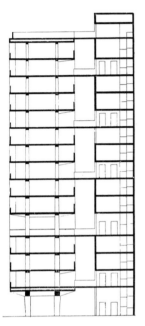

duplex: lower floor

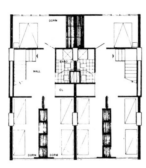

duplex: upper floor

simplex

28 Guido BERMUDEZ
UNIDAD DE HABITACIÓN
CERRO GRANDE, EL VALLE, CARACAS, VENEZUELA. 1951-54

As its very name indicates, this block of apartments built by the Banco Obrero, the Venezuelan housing authority, is inspired by Le Corbusier's Unité d'Habitation at Marseilles. But the actual organization of the ranges of two-storey maisonettes and their external expression is more like Powell and Moya's De Quincey House in London. On the front the skillful variation in the sash sizes — and even their color — suggests the internal complexity of the two-storeyed dwelling units and helps to retain a domestic scale within the monumental scale of the block as a whole. On the rear the freestanding elevator towers, linked by bridges to the galleries of access, offer a bolder and more dramatic sort of composition. The range of shops, coming forward at right angles, is more conveniently located for public access than Le Corbusier's at Marseilles, and justifies the community idea implicit in the term *Unidad*.

29 Guido BERMÚDEZ, J. Centellas, C. A. Brando, José Hoffmann, José Manuel Mijares,
J. A. Ruig Madriz, J. Noriega; Carlos Raúl Villanueva, consultant
MULTICELULARES, CERRO PILOTO (CERRO PILOTO HOUSING DEVELOPMENT) CARACAS, VENEZUELA. 1954

The Cerro Piloto development on the edges of the world's most rapidly expanding city is the most ambitious work to date of the Banco Obrero, the State Housing Authority. It is also one of the largest in the world, including forty-eight blocks, and represents a unique feat of rapid construction, particularly in Latin America, the first third of the program having been completed within a single year. Intended in the main to rehouse new arrivals in the area whose shacks have spread over the surrounding hills, the apartments are very modest in finish. But the plans incorporate with great ingenuity dwelling units of many different sizes serviced by skip-floor elevators. Construction is rather rough and ready but standardization has allowed serial production of the blocks and the colored rendering happily continues a Venezuelan tradition. The wooded mountains serve as a splendid background for the very tall blocks and the rising terrain on both sides of the valley has necessitated much variety in the grouping of the nearly identical blocks. Wide spacing generally provides magnificent views from all windows and the finish, inside and out, if rather crude is at least direct and unpretentious. The scale and pace of the operation justify on the whole the lack of finish in the execution. The result seems almost the equivalent of a complete city and the vision of these loose groups of blocks set against the splendid landscape seems to realize one of the recurrent dreams of twentieth century urbanism.

site plan

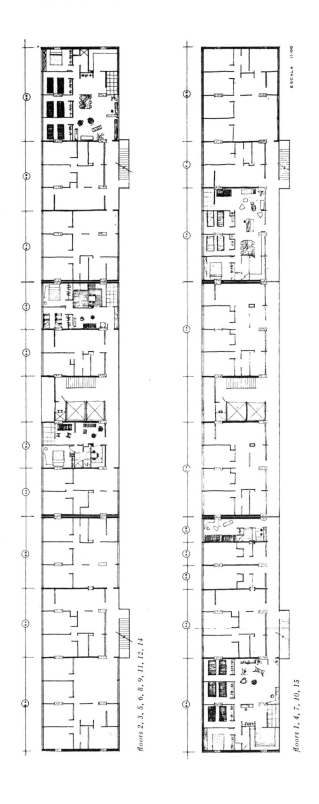

ESCALA 1:100

floors 2, 3, 5, 6, 8, 9, 11, 12, 14

floors 1, 4, 7, 10, 15

section

139

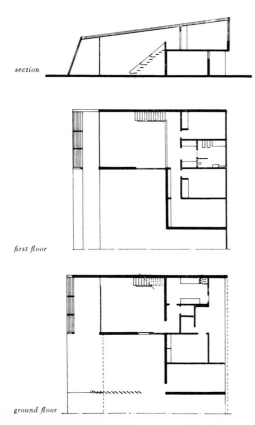

section

first floor

ground floor

30 Oscar NIEMEYER Soares Filho
STAFF HOUSING, CENTRO TÉCNICO DE AERONAUTICA.
SÃO JOSÉ DOS CAMPOS, BRAZIL. 1947-48

In 1947 Niemeyer planned a most elaborate aeronautical training school for the Brazilian government. Of the principal buildings which will house the training activities only a few are completed, but quite extensive ranges of housing for the staff and personnel provide the equivalent of a considerable public housing development. Under the discipline of producing economically various types of modest serial dwellings, Niemeyer has restrained his more virtuoso talents and displayed instead his ability to give, with a remarkable economy of means, interest and architectural quality not only to the individual units but to the disposition of long ranges of them on a flat and open terrain. The sun control devices are of the simplest yet their varying character gives interest to the groups. Details such as the helical stairs and the yard fences of ordinary hollow tile set endwise lend accent and texture. The larger houses with their slanted screens of lattice and two-storey living rooms follow closely the model of a weekend house Niemeyer built earlier for himself, perhaps as a prototype.

30 NIEMEYER

STAFF HOUSING, SÃO JOSÉ DOS CAMPOS, BRAZIL

31 CUELLAR, SERRANO, GÓMEZ y Cia., Ltda.

CONJUNTO DE CASAS ECONOMICAS (LOW COST HOUSING
DEVELOPMENT)
LA SOLEDAD, CARRERAS 22-26 AND CALLES 39-40,
BOGOTÁ, COLOMBIA. 1952-53

These row houses were built by the Banco Central Hipotecário
for its employees. Quiet and almost English, with their red
brick walls, these ranges of small houses provide a rather unusual sort of middle-class dwelling in Latin America where
there tends to be a very great disparity between the accommo-
dations offered in single large dwellings for the upper classes
and in small apartments for the working class. Individually
these houses with their slightly varying plans have been skillfully combined to form streets of varied interest. Well executed in good materials of sober hue they contrast in their
dignified restraint with the ranges of comparable individual
houses by builders, usually of the flimsiest construction and
covered gaudily with painted stucco, that are rising along the
edges of so many Latin American cities. Untypical of the re-
gion as a whole, they are nonetheless typical of the sobriety
of approach and the high technical competence of Colombian
architects.

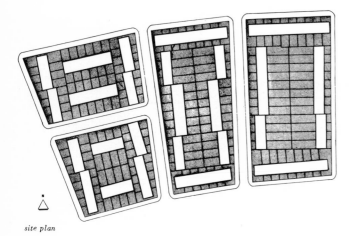

site plan

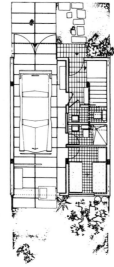

ground floor

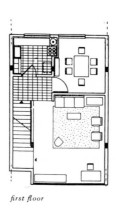

first floor

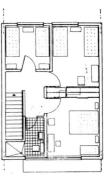

second floor

144

32 Jorge Machado MOREIRA

EDIFICIO ANTONIO CEPPAS (ANTONIO CEPPAS BUILDING)
RUA BENJAMIN BATISTA, RIO DE JANEIRO, BRAZIL. 1952

Lattice grills and movable louvers allow a maximum of ventilation to these apartments while reducing the glazed areas. At eye level on the ground floor *azulejos* designed in the architect's office provide delicately scaled detail. The concrete structural elements are covered with pale tile-mosaic used as a permanent substitute for paint. Like most new Brazilian apartment houses, this is raised off the ground on freestanding concrete supports. Local building codes permit an extra storey at the top when the ground storey is not utilized and thus encourage this characteristic treatment.

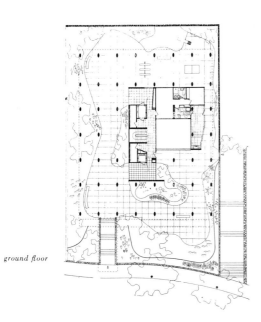

typical floor

32 MOREIRA
EDIFICIO ANTONIO CEPPAS, RIO DE JANEIRO, BRAZIL

ground floor

149

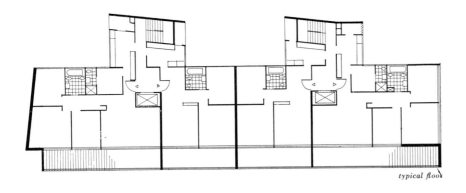

typical floor

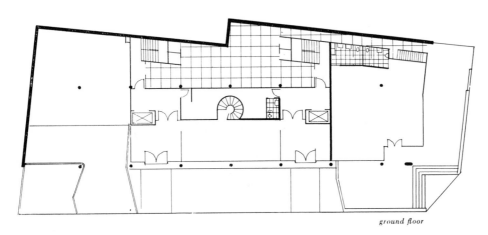

ground floor

33 Raúl A. SICHERO BOURET
EDIFICIOS RAMBLA Y GUAYAQUÍ (RAMBLA AND GUAYAQUÍ
APARTMENT HOUSES)
RAMBLA REPUBLICA DEL PERÚ AT CALLE GUAYAQUÍ,
MONTEVIDEO, URUGUAY. 1952

The new apartment houses along the beach at Montevideo are still but a handful compared to the solid wall they form around Copacabana Bay at Rio. The best of them, however, have a lightness and directness of expression not found at Copacabana. Projecting terrace slabs and vertical louvers of varnished hardwood provide sun control toward the sea, the louvers varying in position because of the alternation in the apartment plans on successive floors. The butterfly roof of the architect's penthouse, accented by the round towers for the elevator machinery, varies the rectangular silhouette of the block. Sichero's detailing, although very simple, is always elegant and the quality of execution is excellent.

151

34 Lucio COSTA

EDIFICIOS NOVA CINTRA, BRISTOL, AND NOVA CALEDONIA,
(NOVA CINTRA, BRISTOL, AND NOVA CALEDONIA
APARTMENT HOUSES)
RUA CAGO CONTINHO, AND RUA DR. PAULO CESAR DE
ANDRADE, PARQUE GUINLE, RIO DE JANEIRO, BRAZIL. 1947-53

This range of apartment blocks rising along the northern edge of the Parque Guinle — two more are intended to be built to the west — is one of the most characteristic and successful examples of Cariocan architecture. By using different types of sun control — both vertical louvers and grills of tile to provide a happy combination of regularity and variety — Costa has expressed with unusual clarity on the exterior the individuality of the dwelling units within. He has also avoided the inhuman scale and monotonous detailing of most modern apartment houses. The pleasant light colors stand out effectively against the background of dark trees and rocks, and are not inappropriate to the delicacy of the membering throughout. First begun almost a decade ago, the design of these blocks has had a wide influence in Brazil and in other countries.

typical floor

34 Lucio COSTA

EDIFICIOS NOVA CINTRA, BRISTOL, AND NOVA CALEDONIA
(NOVA CINTRA, BRISTOL, AND NOVA CALEDONIA
APARTMENT HOUSES)
RUA GAGO COUTINHO, AND RUA DR. PAULO CESAR DE
ANDRADE, PARQUE GUINLE, RIO DE JANEIRO, BRAZIL. 1947-53

35 GUINAND y BENACERRAF — Roger Halle
EDIFICIO MONTSERRAT (MONTSERRAT APARTMENT BUILDING)
PLAZA ALTAMIRA, ALTAMIRA, CARÁCAS, VENEZUELA. 1950

This small block of luxurious one-room apartments is skillfully planned, providing in each unit a well articulated spatial complex. Brazilian ideas appear in the handling of the tile grill, but the total effect is more solid if somewhat less gracious than Costa's and Moreira's Rio apartment houses. Apartments are still something of a novelty in Caracas, however, and most of those so far built are commonplace in design and tawdry in execution.

typical floor

36 LE CORBUSIER

HOUSE FOR DR. PEDRO D. CURUCHET
LA PLATA, ARGENTINA. 1949-54

Although Le Corbusier has probably had more influence in
Latin America than any other European architect, it is surprising to note how different this house is from the houses
built by local architects. On a relatively narrow urban lot
framed by party walls, the European architect has created a
sort of space-cage open at the base and criss-crossed by ramps
leading up to the doctor's office in front and the vestibule of
the dwelling to the rear. The dwelling itself is a two-storey
maisonette opening on its own terrace at tree-top level. Such
complex spatial play is rare in Latin America; on the other
hand the apartment-like planning of the actual dwelling makes
evident the greater generosity and openness of native Latin
American house-planning.

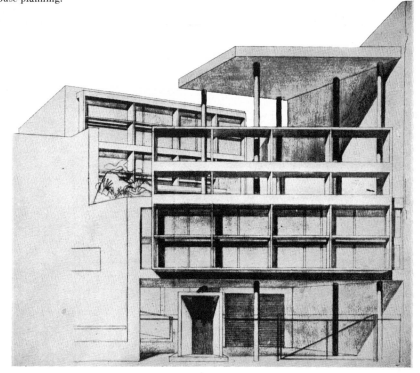

36 LE CORBUSIER

HOUSE FOR DR. PEDRO D. CURUCHET, LA PLATA, ARGENTINA

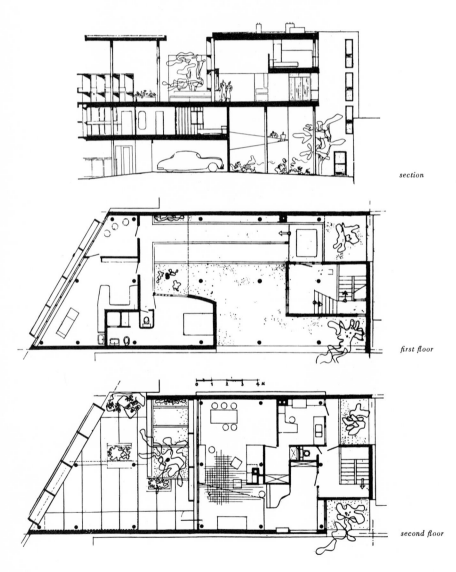

section

first floor

second floor

37 Antonio BONET

HOUSE FOR GABRIEL BERLINGIERI. PUNTA BALLENA, URUGUAY.
1946-47

Low-pitched shell vaults, usually associated with much larger
buildings, give special character to this seaside house. Ingenious use is made of the rising terrain to the right to place
the one-storeyed bedroom wing on a level with the balcony of
the two-storeyed living room. Tile grills partially closing in
the bedroom corridor and the long wooden veranda boldly
cantilevered across the front of the main block contract pleas-
antly with rendered members of the concrete frame. Avoiding
the established clichés of contemporary house design, Bonet
seems to have been influenced by an exceptional Le Corbusier
house built in the 1930s near Chantilly. Although the house
is in Uruguay and Bonet is Spanish-born, the Punta Ballena
development was planned entirely for Argentines and this must
be considered an example of Argentine rather than Uruguayan
architecture.

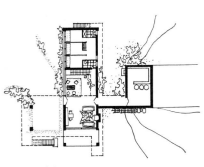

ground floor

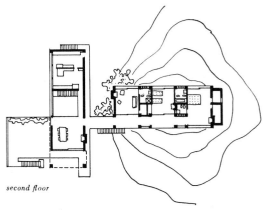

second floor

38 Amancio WILLIAMS

HOUSE FOR ALBERTO WILLIAMS, PARQUE PEREYRA IRAOLA, MAR DEL PLATA, ARGENTINA. 1945-47

By a bold structural device this striking house makes the most of a declivity in the park-like site. A bridge-like curved slab carries the whole house, its simple but unusual forms very directly detailed in exposed concrete. The narrow oblong of the plan, with bedrooms on one side and living area on the other, seems somewhat restricted, but the continuity of interior space and the unbroken range of the windowband, opening into the tree tops, are notable, as is the compact conception of the entire edifice, as compared with most other Latin American work built in the past decade.

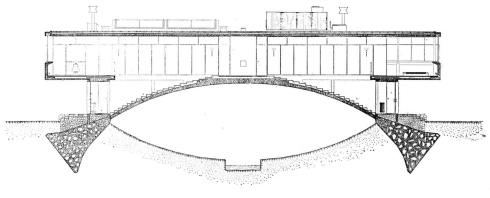

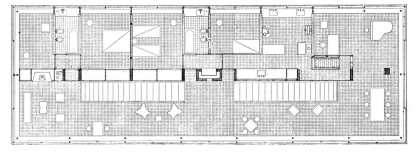

165

39 Jorge COSTABAL

HOUSE FOR JUAN COSTABAL
CALLE O'BRIEN, 2829, VITACURA, LAS CONDES,
SANTIAGO, CHILE. 1945-55

This small house, isolated from the street by its own walled patio and open beyond its rear garden to the mountains, illustrates the increasingly disciplined approach of many of the younger architects of Latin America, both as regards restraint in formal organization and a sturdily structural expression of the ferro-concrete frame. Supports are solidly scaled, slabs are not mere planes but have visible thickness, yet the careful adjustment of the proportions avoids, even in so small an edifice, any effect of heaviness. The articulation of the main living space by varying the floor level is somewhat arbitrary but clearly organized. Conceptually the layout of the plan with service and garage to the right of the patio and bedrooms to the left is also logical. From the street there is plenty of both real and psychological protection, yet the lowered slab over the entrance-way focuses attention on the front door and draws the visitor in.

40 Oscar NIEMEYER Soares Filho
HOUSE FOR OSCAR NIEMEYER SOARES FILHO.
ESTRADA DOS CANOAS, 2350, GÁVEA,
RIO DE JANEIRO, BRAZIL. 1953-54

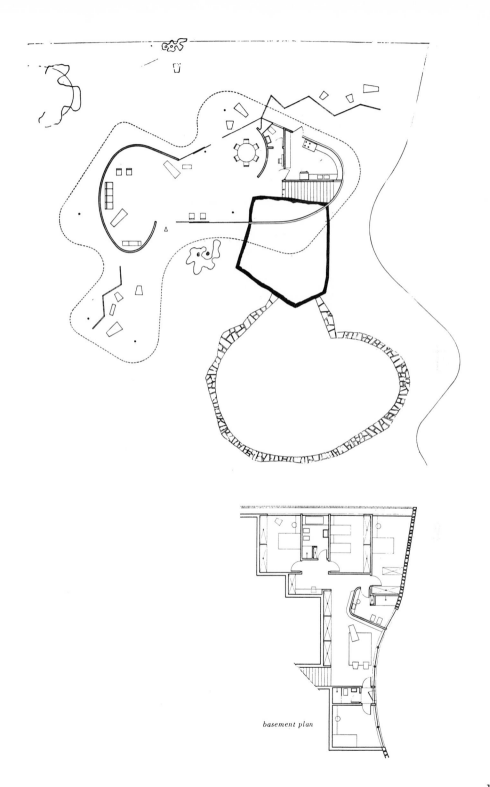

basement plan

40 Oscar NIEMEYER Soares Filho
HOUSE FOR OSCAR NIEMEYER SOARES FILHO.
ESTRADA DOS CANOAS, 2350, GÁVEA,
RIO DE JANEIRO, BRAZIL. 1953-54

Quite properly Niemeyer's own house is the most extreme state-
ment of his special Cariocan lyricism. Set in the hills high
above the superb Bay of Gávea, the special harmony he seeks
between the boldly rounded outlines of the hills and the sinuous
curves of his plans is very evident here. Approached from
above, the interlocked "free forms" of the pavilion roof and
the swimming pool are seen in the foreground against the
ocean and the headlands beyond. At terrace level, the pavilion
is so completely open that the view carries right through between the two more solidly walled ends, the crisp straight line
of the terrace railing providing a simple base line for the landscape. The pavilion contains only the main living areas and
the kitchen. All other facilities are hidden away below the
terrace with no relationship at all to the pavilion on top. Only,
perhaps, its own designer and his family would find this an
altogether comfortable residence; but as an expression of lyri-
cal response to landscape it is unique in the modern world and
powerful evidence of Niemeyer's continued creativity.

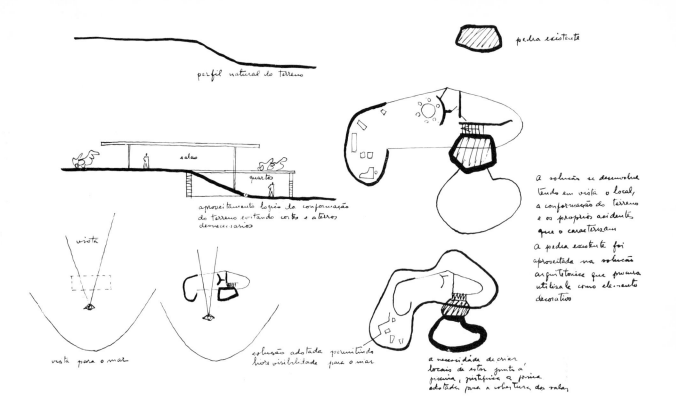

perfil natural do terreno

pedra existente

salas

quartos

aproveitamento logico da conformação
do terreno evitando cortes e aterros
desnecessarios

vista

vista para o mar

solução adotada permitindo
livre visibilidade para o mar

a solução se desenvolve
tendo em vista o local,
a conformação do terreno
e os proprios acidentes
que o caracterisam
a pedra existente foi
aproveitada na solução
arquitetonica que procura
utilisa-la como elemento
decorativo

a necessidade de criar
locais de estar junto á
piscina, justifica a forma
adotada para a cobertura das salas

41 Henrique Ephim MINDLIN
HOUSE FOR GEORGE HIME. BOMCLIMA, NEAR PETRÓPOLIS, BRAZIL. 1950

172

The sharp separation in expression between the main living areas to the left and the bedroom wing with its continuous ranges of jalousied windows makes very plain the difference in balance of parts between modern houses in the States and in Latin America. Large families and plentiful servants require extensive bedroom and service facilities. In the interior the exploitation of vertical space, with the living areas on three different levels connected by open stairs is most dramatic. Vista is everywhere consciously emphasized. The rising slope of the garden — originally laid out by Roberto Burle-Marx — provides a backdrop for the living terrace beneath the bedroom wing. Opposite the entrance on the landing a large Calder mobile animates the open well between sitting room and dining room. At the other end of the house a curved freestanding wall with a Burle-Marx mosaic closes the view along the terrace in that direction. The local rubble of delicate scale used for the tall sitting room wall and for the retaining wall which comes right in through the glazed side of the living space provides excellent textural contrast to the characteristic stucco.

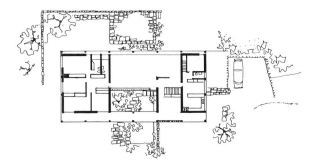

Two things are especially striking about this house: on the one hand its highly ordered geometry within the visible frame of ferro-concrete supports and slabs; on the other hand its apparent lack of those defences against the outer world which close in most Latin American houses, old or new. (Actually the concrete grills on the west provide protection against marauders, as well as effective sun control, and on the other side a simple but sturdy screen of iron bars can be drawn across the glass wall of the living room). This architect's approach to form and to visible expression of structure is consciously Miesian, but through his choice of materials and in such detailing as the screens of precast concrete elements he arrives at a quite personal effect. Located high on the hills to the west of São Paulo, the view is most important here; therefore, except for the lush planting at the pool that cuts into the rectangle of the plan on the west of the house, the setting is kept open and the house tells as a formal artifact in the landscape rather than merging with the natural setting. Toward this effect the visual continuity of the floor slab, lifted slightly off the ground even at the upper end, notably contributes.

42 Osvaldo Arthur BRATKE

HOUSE FOR OSVALDO ARTHUR BRATKE
AVENIDA MORUMBI, 3008, SÃO PAULO, BRAZIL. 1953

43 Sergio Wladimir BERNARDES

HOUSE OF DR. JADIR DE SOUZA
AVENIDA VISCONDE DE ALBUQUERQUE, 971, GÁVEA,
RIO DE JANEIRO, BRAZIL. 1951

Protected from the street by the higher level of the site, this suburban house is so planned that the main living areas open generously on the characteristic garden by Roberto Burle-Marx, while the bedrooms across the front have their own high level terrace and the protection of louvered jalousies. The variety of materials here — little painted stucco and much surprisingly good brickwork and varnished hardwood — is novel in Brazil. Although the butterfly roof is Cariocan, this is not visible from the street, and the crisp rectangularity of most of the design presumably represents, as in Bratke's house, a mild reaction against the curves and oblique lines of so much Brazilian building. The choice of materials, eschewing the artificial polychromy of painted stucco and *azulejos*, illustrates a conscious search for better craftsmanship and, in general, a less abstract approach to architecture than that with which the Cariocan school began.

section

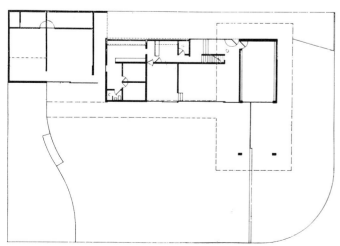

plan at ground level

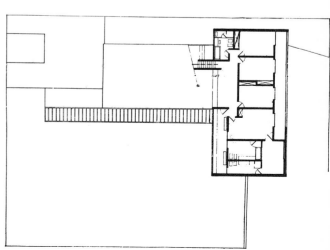

first floor

44 Juan SORDO MADALENO

HOUSE FOR JUAN SORDO MADALENO. PASEO DE LA REFORMA, 2388, LOMAS DE CHAPULTEPEC, MEXICO, D.F. 1951-52

This large suburban house, almost in the country, well illustrates the special approach of Mexican architects in designing houses. Beyond the solid wall that flanks the road one enters a forecourt, in this case at a higher level than the rest of the site. Two freestanding blank walls, one brown, one blue, with a great bronze crucifix by Mathias Goeritz on one, define a space that is almost monumental. Descending behind one of the screen walls the visitor comes out beside the swimming pool, roofed at the inner end but extending out into the garden beyond. The garden, large and loosely articulated by varied planting, provides the general living area of the house. Covered terraces at garden level make a transition to the actual enclosed rooms in the main block of the house which is set against the rising ground toward the street. A smaller patio provides additional light to the inner range of rooms. Careful proportions, well chosen materials, and excellent execution provide settings of rather formal dignity. But the architectural elements are but the backdrop, as it were, to the house as a place to live which has its real focus in the garden.

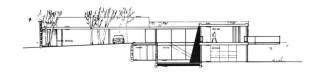

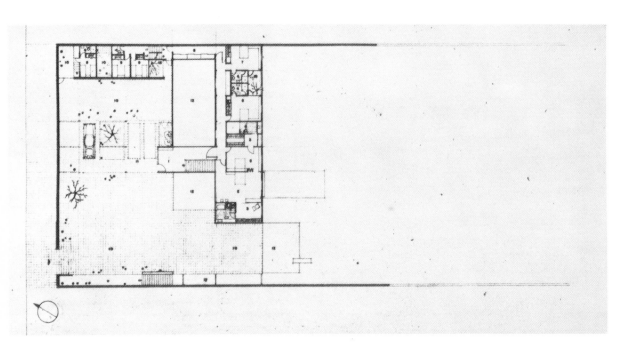

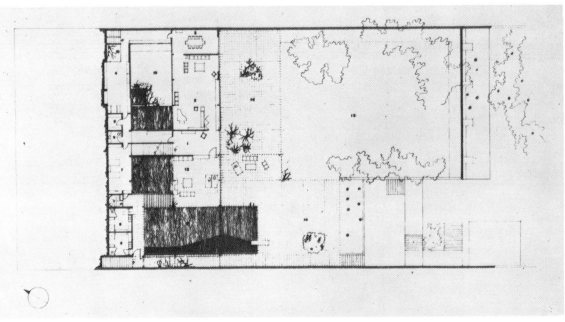

44 SORDO MADALENO
HOUSE FOR JUAN SORDO MADALENO. MEXICO, D.F. 1951-52

45 Luis BARRAGÁN

HOUSE FOR LUIS BARRAGÁN. CALLE GENERAL FRANCISCO RAMÍREZ, 14,
TACUBAYA, MEXICO, D.F. 1948

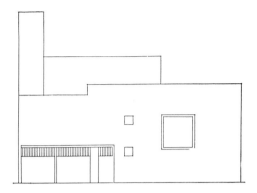

street facade

This house has, in effect, no exterior. The almost blank street façade is hardly distinguishable from its older neighbors and on the garden side the rich planting frames the great window of the living room and largely masks the surrounding walls. Barragán's vocabulary derives hardly at all from international modern architecture. Traditional in its materials, sturdy in its scaling, his architecture represents a most sophisticated handling of Mexican provincial building methods. But the effects he achieves so simply, as in the walled roof terrace, have a strong and highly conscious abstract quality. The spatial values of the interiors, some tall and complex, others lower and plainer, are notably original also; his staircases in particular achieve with the most outstanding rudimentary means a most positive sort of visual drama. Not trained as an architect, indeed with no technical training at all, Barragán here and in the layout of the Jardines de Pedregal subdivision illustrates a highly personal talent that has not been without influence on other Mexican architects.

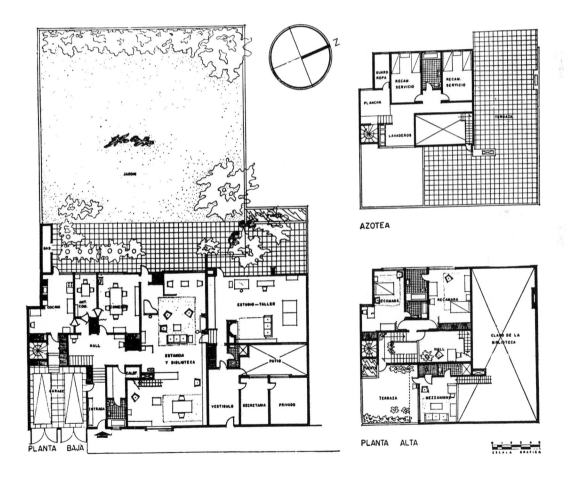

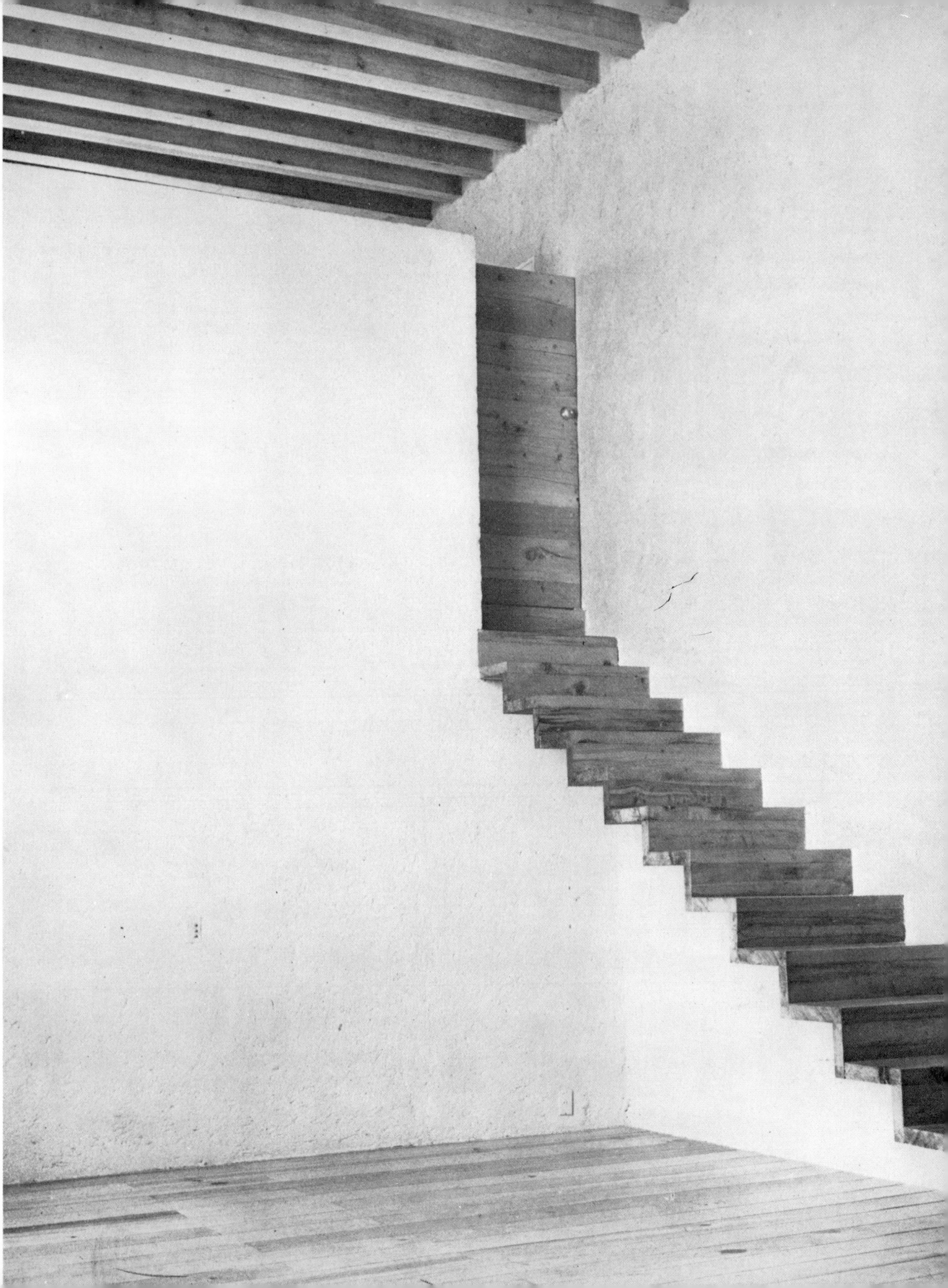

45 BARRAGÁN HOUSE FOR LUIS BARRAGÁN. MEXICO, D.F.

46 Francisco ARTIGAS

HOUSE FOR SRA. CARMEN DEL OLMO DE ARTIGAS
PRIOR 32, SAN ÁNGEL, MEXICO, D.F. 1953

This house recalls a little the Mies "court" house projects of
twenty years ago. But the setting under the magnificent trees
of an old private park produces a wholly different effect. It
will be noted that there is no definite living room; the garden
itself between the garage and office range along the street and
the domestic range to the rear provides the principal living
area. The light pavilion-like structure of the two ranges is
crisp and precise, happily contrasting with the lush forms of
the foliage. Characteristically the house offers to the street
nothing more than a blank wall.

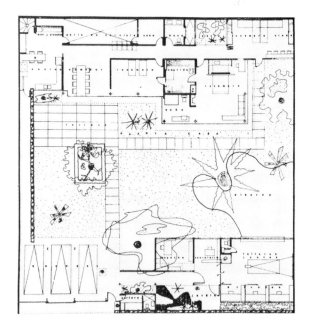

47 Emilio DUHART H.

HOUSE FOR SRA. MARTA H. DE DUHART
AVENIDA VATICANO 78, SANTIAGO, CHILE. 1946

Although its thin membering and crisp definition reflects the architect's experience with Gropius and with Pei in the States, the planning is definitely Latin American. The nearly blank front wall rises at the sidewalk's edge and the L-shaped plan provides for main living areas across the front with service and bedrooms to the rear, all opening on a high-fenced garden. The way the space of the living room seems to be defined not by its glazed end but by the wall beyond, thus incorporating the pool and its surrounding foliage visually in the living area, is especially successful. The precision of the designing and the excellent execution would be notable anywhere, while the pebble-covered outer wall introduces a textural interest delicately scaled to the slightness and smoothness of all the other elements.

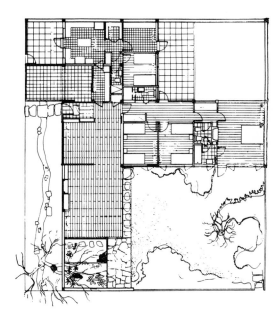

Urban Façades (photographs pages 192-197)

The strikingly contemporary air of most Latin American cities is above all due to the presence of great numbers of new office buildings, and in some cases, apartment blocks, rising above the generally low urban structures of earlier periods. There are many varieties of façade treatment, from the flat fronts of alternating horizontal strips of window and cement- or stone-faced spandrel, of an order increasingly common all over the world since the late 1920s, to the strong patterns of horizontal or vertical sunbreaks that are a Latin American specialty. In A, the flat front is bent into a somewhat Baroque double curve. In B, descending mullions phrase the spandrels with the sash above them. In C, the projection of the banded outer plane in front of the main structural system is made clearly evident above and below and at the edges. In D, flat bands are combined with projecting balcony slabs, thus clearly distinguishing the apartment bedrooms and such from the living rooms with their recessed all-glass walls.

More and more, articulated types of façades are superseding the flatter mode inherited from the 1920s. In E, the elegantly finished concrete structural frame stands forward of the window plane. In F and in J, a crate-like grid with movable louvers provides adjustable sun-control. Fixed horizontal louvers in G and movable vertical louvers in H give a new sort of scale, in the case of G perhaps too confusing because of the total obscuration of the storey lines. I and K show different treatment of balconies on apartment houses, the former providing considerable sun protection, the latter more purely a means of creating plastic variety in the wall plane.

But ferro-concrete construction in Latin America, almost as much as steel construction in the United States, has encouraged also the sheathing of buildings with various combinations of glass and opaque panels mounted in continuous metal chassis-frames. For a discussion of L, certainly the finest example, see page 115. M, N, O and P are very similar to each other, but in M the emphasis is more horizontal because of the slightly projecting members at the storey lines, while in P it is more vertical because of the rather narrow spacing of the continuous mullions. Altogether a surprisingly wide range of façade treatments are being developed, of course with varying individual success, within a consistent contemporary stylistic frame; as a result the current rebuilding of Latin American cities has in general produced an over-all harmony of character without the monotony that might have been feared.

A

B

C

A   J. M. MONTOYA VALENZUELA: OFFICE BUILDING, CALLE 13 BETWEEN CARRERAS 6A AND 7A, BOGOTÁ, COLOMBIA, 1948

B   RAFAEL R. GRAZIANI; LUIS R. Y LUIS J. GRAZIANI: EDIFICIO E.M.S.A., SAN MARTÍN 627, BUENOS AIRES, ARGENTINA, 1951

C   CUELLAR, SERRANO, GÓMEZ Y CIA: EDIFICIO COLÓN, BOGOTÁ, COLOMBIA, 1952-53

D

E

D   JORGE FERRARI HARDOY: APARTMENT HOUSE, AVENIDA PRESIDENTE FIGUEROA ALCORTA 3492-3500, BUENOS AIRES, ARGENTINA, 1953-54

E   BRUNO VIOLI: EDIFICIO SMIDT, CARRERA 7A, NO. 11-53, BOGOTÁ, COLOMBIA, 1951

F LUCJAN KORNGOLD: EDIFICIO C.B.I., PRAÇA RAMOS DE AZEVEDO 206, 8 ANDAR, SÃO PAULO, BRAZIL, 1948-51

G ANTONIO QUINTANA SIMONETTI; MANUEL A. RUBIO; AUGUSTO PÉREZ BEATO: RETIRO ODONTOLÓGICO, CALLE L NO. 353, HAVANA, CUBA, 1953-54

H GUSTAVO MORENO LÓPEZ: EDIFICIOS MISIONES, AVENIDA DE LAS MISIONES 25-29, HAVANA, CUBA, 1951-52

I   J   K

I   ENRIQUE SEOANE ROS: EDIFICIO NAZARENAS, APARTMENT HOUSE, AVENIDA TACNA, LIMA, PERU, 1952-54

J   LUIS MIGUEL MOREA; PATER Y MOREA: EDIFICIO ESSO, AVENIDA BELGRANO 8015, BUENOS AIRES, ARGENTINA, 1915-51

K   HENRIQUE EPHÍM MINDLIN: EDIFICIO TRES LEÕES, AVENIDA SÃO JOÃO 1072/1116, SÃO PAULO, BRAZIL, 1951

L   VEGAS Y GALIA: EDIFICIO POLAR, PLAZA VENEZUELA, CARACAS, VENEZUELA, 1953-54

M   RINO LEVI: BANCO PAULISTA DO COMERCIO RUA BOA VISTA AT LADEIRA PORTO GERAL, SÃO PAULO, BRAZIL, 1947-48

N   JUAN SORDO MADALENO: OFFICE BUILDING, CALLE DE NIZA AT CALLE DE LONDRES, MEXICO, D.F., 1952-53

O   LUIS MIRO QUESADA GARLAND: EDIFICIO RADIO EL SOL, AVENIDA VENEZUELA 351, LIMA, PERU, 1953-54

P   CUELLAR, SERRANO, GÓMEZ Y CIA: EDIFICIO DE LA CIA. SURAMERICANA DE SEGUROS, AVENIDA JIMÉNEZ DE QUESADA BETWEEN
    CARRERAS 8 AND 9, BOGOTÁ, COLOMBIA, 1954

BIOGRAPHIES OF ARCHITECTS

ABRAMOVITZ, Max (see also Harrison and Abramovitz)
Born: Chicago, Illinois, 1908
Studied: University of Illinois, Urbana; Columbia University,
  New York
Address: 630 Fifth Avenue, New York

AGURTO Calvo, Santiago
Born: Guayaquil, Peru, 1921
Studied: Escuela Nacional de Ingenieros, Lima;
  Cornell University, Ithaca, N. Y.
Address: Colmena 530, Oficina 503, Lima, Peru

ARTIGAS, Francisco
Born: Mexico, D.F., 1916
Studied: Universidad Nacional de México
Address: Prior 32, San Ángel, Mexico, D.F.

BARRAGÁN, Luis
Born: Guadalajara, Mexico, 1902
Address: General Francisco Ramírez 14, Tacubaya,
  Mexico, D.F.

BENACERRAF, Moisés F.
Born: Caracas, Venezuela, 1924
Studied: Yale University, New Haven, Conn.
Address: Puente Yanez a Tracabordo, Caracas, Venezuela

BERMÚDEZ, Guido
Born: Maraiaito, Venezuela, 1925
Studied: Universidad Central, Caracas
Address: Edificio Carpa, Apt. 12, Altamira. Caracas, Venezuela

BERNARDES, Sergio Wladimir
Born: Rio de Janeiro, Brazil, 1919
Studied: Universidade do Brasil, Rio de Janeiro
Address: Rua Senador Dantas 74, 11 Andar,
  Rio de Janeiro, Brazil

BIANCO, Mario
Born: Varello (Provincia di Vercelli), Italy, 1903
Studied: Istituto Politecnico, Turin, Italy
Address: Tiron Huancavélica 470/409, Lima, Peru

BONET, Antonio
Born: Barcelona, Spain, 1913
Studied: Escuela de Arquitectura de Barcelona
Address: Santa Fé 2656, Piso 9, Departamento B,
  Buenos Aires, Argentina

BORGES, Max, Jr.
Born: Havana, Cuba, 1918
Studied: Georgia Institute of Technology, Atlanta;
  Harvard University, Cambridge, Mass.
Address: Ayestáran y Domínguez, Cerro, Havana, Cuba

BRATKE, Osvaldo Arthur
Born: Botucatú, São Paulo, Brazil, 1907
Studied: Universidade Mackenzie, São Paulo
Address: Rua Avanhandava 136, São Paulo, Brazil

CANDELA, Félix
Born: Madrid, Spain, 1910
Studied: Universidad de Madrid
Address: Ramón Guzmán 123-204, Mexico, D.F.

CAPABLANCA y Graupera, Aquiles
Born: Havana, Cuba, 1907
Studied: Universidad de la Habana
Address: Edificio Banco Nova Scotia 222, Havana, Cuba

CETTO, Max
Born: Coblenz, Germany, 1903
Studied: Technische Hochschule, Munich;
  Technische Hochschule, Berlin
Address: Calle del Agua 130, Jardines de Pedregal,
  Mexico, D.F.

COSTA, Lucio
Born: Toulon, France, 1902
Studied: Escola Nacional de Belas Artes, Rio de Janeiro
Address: Serviço do Pâtrimonio Histórico e Artístico Nacional,
  Ministerio de Educação, Rio de Janeiro, Brazil

COSTABAL, Jorge
Born: Santiago, Chile, 1918
Studied: Universidad Católica, Santiago, Chile
Address: Coronel 2327, Los Leones, Santiago, Chile

CUELLAR, SERRANO, GÓMEZ y Cia., Ltda.
Camilo Cuellar Tamayo
Gabriel Serrano Camargo (see also Serrano Camargo, Gabriel)
José Gómez Pinzón
Gabriel Largacha Manrique
Ernesto Cuellar Tamayo
Address: Edificio Caja Colombiana de Ahorros, Piso 12;
  or Apartado Aéreo 3527, Bogotá, Colombia

DE LA MORA y Palomar, Enrique
Born: Guadalajara, Mexico, 1907
Studied: Universidad Nacional de Mexico
Address: 16 de Septiembre 38, Mexico, D.F.

DE ROBINA, Ricardo
Born: Mexico, D.F., 1919
Studied: Escuela Nacional de Arquitectura,
  Universidad Nacional de Mexico
Address: Oaxaca 37, Mexico, D.F.

DE ROUX, Guillermo
Born: Panama, Republic of Panama, 1916
Studied: University of Virginia, Charlottesville;
   Yale University, New Haven, Conn.
Address: Apartado 1740, Panama, Republic of Panama

DUHART H., Emilio
Born: Temuco, Chile
Studied: Universidad Católica, Santiago, Chile
Address: Calle Miguel de la Barre 536, Santiago, Chile

FERRER, Miguel (see also Toro-Ferrer)
Born: San Juan, Puerto Rico, 1915
Studied: Cornell University, Ithaca, N. Y.
Address: Monserrat 560, Santurce, San Juan, Puerto Rico

GALIA, José Miguel (see also Vegas y Galia)
Born: Caracas, Venezuela, 1926
Studied: Illinois Institute of Technology, Chicago
Address: Edificio Polar, Plaza Venezuela, Caracas, Venezuela

GUINAND, Carlos G.
Born: Caracas, Venezuela, 1925
Studied: Universidad Central, Caracas; Harvard University,
   Cambridge, Mass.
Address: Puente Yanez a Tracabordo, Caracas, Venezuela

HARRISON and ABRAMOVITZ (see also Abramovitz, Max;
   Harrison, Wallace K.)
Address: 630 Fifth Avenue, New York, N. Y.

HARRISON, Wallace K.
Born: Worcester, Mass., 1895
Studied: Ecole de Beaux Arts, Paris
Address: 630 Fifth Avenue, New York, N. Y.

KLUMB, Henry
Born: Cologne, Germany, 1905
Studied: Hohe Technische Bauschule, Cologne;
   Taliesin Fellowship
Address: Apartado 4545, San Juan, Puerto Rico

LE CORBUSIER, Charles-Edouard Jeanneret
Born: La Chaux de Fond, Switzerland
Address: 35 rue de Sévres, Paris, France

LEVI, Rino
Born: São Paulo, Brazil, 1901
Studied: Universitá di Roma, Rome, Italy
Address: Rua Bento Freitas 306, 7 Andar, São Paulo, Brazil

MELLO, Icaro de Castro
Born: São Vicente, Brazil, 1913
Studied: Escola de Engenharia Mackenzie, São Paulo;
   Universidade de São Paulo
Address: Rua Bento Freitas 306, São Paulo, Brazil

MINDLIN, Henrique Ephim
Born: São Paulo, Brazil, 1911
Studied: Escola de Engenharia Mackenzie, São Paulo, Brazil
Address: Avenida Nila Peçanha 12, 9 Andar,
   Rio de Janeiro, Brazil

MOREIRA, Jorge Machado
Born: Paris, France, 1904
Studied: Escola Nacional de Belas Artes, Rio de Janeiro
Address: Escritorio Technico da Cidade Universitaria,
   Ministerio da Fazenda, Rio de Janeiro, Brazil

NIEMEYER Soares Filho, Oscar
Born: Rio de Janeiro, Brazil, 1907
Studied: Escola Nacional de Belas Artes, Rio de Janeiro
Address: Avenida Atlántica 3940, 10 Andar,
   Rio de Janeiro, Brazil

O'GORMAN, Juan
Born: Coyoacán, D.F., Mexico
Studied: Escuela Nacional de Arquitectura,
   Universidad Nacional de México
Address: Calle del Jardin 88, Mexico, D.F.

ORTIZ MONASTERIO, Jaime
Born: Mexico D.F., 1928
Studied: Escuela Nacional de Arquitectura,
   Universidad Nacional de México
Address: Oaxaca 37, Mexico, D.F.

PANI, Mario
Born: Mexico, D.F., 1911
Studied: Ecole des Beaux Arts, Paris, France
Address: Paseo de la Reforma 503, Mexico, D.F.

PÉREZ PALACIOS, Augusto
Born: Mexico, D.F., 1909
Studied: Universidad Nacional de Mexico
Address: Ejército Nacional 678, Mexico, D.F.

PIZANO, Francisco
Born: Paris, France, 1926
Studied: Universidad Nacional, Bogotá; University of
   Michigan, Ann Arbor
Address: Carrera 7, No. 17-64, Bogotá, Colombia

PRIETO, Alejandro
Born: Mexico, D.F., 1924
Studied: Universidad Nacional de Mexico
Address: Calle de Damas 118, San José Insurgentes,
   Mexico, D.F.

REIDY, Affonso Eduardo
Born: Paris, France, 1909
Studied: Escola Nacional de Belas Artes, Rio de Janeiro
Address: Rua Capitão Félix, Pedregulho,
   Rio de Janeiro, Brazil

SERRANO Camargo, Gabriel
Born: Sogamoso, Boyacá, Colombia, 1908
Studied: Universidad Nacional, Bogotá
Address: Cuellar, Serrano, Gómez y Cia., Ltda., Edificio Caja
   Colombiana de Ahorros, Piso 12, Bogotá, Colombia

SICHERO BOURET, Raúl A.
Born: Rivera, Uruguay, 1916
Studied: Universidad de Montevideo
Address: Rambla República del Peru 1081,
   Montevideo, Uruguay

SOLANO, Mesa Gabriel
Born: Duitama, Colombia, 1916
Studied: Universidad Nacional, Bogotá; University of Penn-
   sylvania, Philadelphia; Harvard University, Cambridge,
   Mass.
Address: Avenida Jiménez de Oacada, No. 7-25,
   Bogotá, Colombia

SORDO MADALENO, Juan
Born: Mexico, D.F., 1916
Studied: Universidad Nacional de México
Address: Avenida Morelos 110, Mexico, D.F.

TORO-FERRER (see also Toro, Osvaldo Luis;
   Ferrer, Miguel)
Address: Monserrat 560, Santurce, San Juan, Puerto Rico

TORO, Osvaldo Luis
Born: San Juan, Puerto Rico, 1914
Studied: Columbia University, New York
Address: Monserrat 560, Santurce, San Juan, Puerto Rico

VEGAS Y GALIA (see also Galia, José Miguel)
   Martín Vegas Pacheco
   José Miguel Galia
Address: Edificio Polar, Plaza Venezuela, Caracas, Venezuela

VILLANUEVA, Carlos Raúl
Born: Croydon, England, 1900
Studied: Ecole des Beaux Arts, Paris
Address: Los Jabillos 27, La Florida, Caracas, Venezuela

WILLIAMS, Amancio
Born: Buenos Aires, Argentina, 1913
Studied: Universidad de Buenos Aires
Address: 11 de Septiembre No. 1500, Belgrano,
   Buenos Aires, Argentina

INDEX OF ARCHITECTS

Architects are listed alphabetically by the countries in which they work.

PUERTO RICO

FERRER, Miguel (Toro-Ferrer)
HOUSE FOR TEODORO MOSCOSO
  Santurce, 1950   *p.59*
..... (Toro, Ferrer y Torregrossa; Warner-Leeds, Interiors)
CARIBE HILTON HOTEL
  San Juan, 1947-49   *pp.120-121*

KLUMB, Henry
IGLESIA DEL BEATO MARTÍN DE PORRES (CHURCH OF THE
BLESSED MARTIN PORRES)
  Bayview, Cataño, near San Juan, 1950   *pp.70-71*
LIBRARY, UNIVERSITY OF PUERTO RICO
  Rio Piedras   *p.58*

TORO, Osvaldo Luis (Toro-Ferrer)
HOUSE FOR TEODORO MOSCOSO
  Santurce, 1950   *p.59*
..... (Toro, Ferrer y Torregrossa; Warner-Leeds, Interiors)
CARIBE HILTON HOTEL
  San Juan, 1947-49   *pp.120-121*

REPUBLIC OF PANAMA

DE ROUX, Guillermo, René Brenes, and Ricardo Bermúdez
ESCUELA DE ADMINISTRACIÓN Y COMERCIO (SCHOOL OF
ADMINISTRATION AND BUSINESS)
  Universidad de Panamá, Panama, 1949-53   *pp.82-83*

STONE, Edward
EL PANAMÁ HOTEL
  Panama City, 1950   *p.24*

URUGUAY

BONET, Antonio
CLUBHOUSE
  Punta Ballena, 1947-48   *p.54*
HOUSE FOR GABRIEL BERLINGIERI
  Punta Ballena, 1946-47   *pp.162-163*

JONES ODRIOZOLO, Guillermo
HOUSE FOR THE ARCHITECT
  Punta Ballena   *p.54*

SICHERO BOURET, Raúl A.
EDIFICIOS RAMBLA Y GUAYAQUÍ (RAMBLA AND GUAYAQUÍ
APARTMENT HOUSES)
  Rambla República del Perú at Calle Guayaquí,
  Montevideo, 1952   *pp.150-151*

VILAMAJÓ, Julio
FACULTY OF ENGINEERING, UNIVERSITY OF THE REPUBLIC
  565 Julio Herrera y Reissig Avenue, Parque Rodo,
  Montevideo, 1937   *p.24*

VENEZUELA

BENACERRAF, Moisés F. (Guinand y Benacerraf —
Roger Halle)
EDIFICIO MONTSERRAT (MONTSERRAT APARTMENT BUILDING)
  Plaza Altamira, Caracas, 1950   *pp.156-157*

BERMÚDEZ, Guido
UNIDAD DE HABITACIÓN
  Cerro Grande, El Valle, Caracas, 1951-54   *pp.134-135*
.....with J. Centellas, C. A. Brando, José Hoffman, José
Manuel Mijares, J. A. Ruig Madriz, J. Noriega; Carlos Raúl
Villanueva, consultant
MULTICELULARES, CERRO PILOTO (CERRO PILOTO HOUSING
DEVELOPMENT)
  Caracas, 1954   *pp.136-139*

GALIA, José Miguel (Vegas y Galia)
EDIFICIO POLAR (POLAR BUILDING)
  Plaza Venezuela, Caracas, 1952-54   *pp.114-117, 196*

GUINAND, Carlos G. (Guinand y Benacerraf — Roger Halle)
EDIFICIO MONTSERRAT (MONTSERRAT APARTMENT BUILDING)
  Plaza Altamira, Caracas, 1950   *pp.156-157*

VEGAS Pacheco, Martín (Vegas y Galia)
EDIFICIO POLAR (POLAR BUILDING)
  Plaza Venezuela, Caracas, 1952-54   *pp.114-117, 196*

VILLANUEVA, Carlos Raúl
AULA MAGNA AND PLAZA CUBIERTA (AUDITORIUM AND
COVERED PLAZA)
  Ciudad Universitaria, Caracas, 1952-53   *pp.50, 51, 78-81*
ESTADIO OLÍMPICO (OLYMPIC STADIUM)
  Ciudad Universitaria, Caracas, 1950-51   *pp.94-97*

Photographer's Credits

Aertsens Michel, Rio de Janeiro, 84, 85, 86, 129 top, 146, 147, 148, 149, 173, 176, 177; C. Arias, Havana, 72, 73; Carlos Botelho, Rio de Janeiro, 34; Brazilian Government Trade Bureau, 38; Hugo Brehme, Mexico, D.F., 14 top, 42; M. Chamudes, Santiago, Chile, 188 bottom; Nicolau Drei, Rio de Janeiro, 168; Foto Industrial, Bogotá, 40, 88, 89, 99, 106, 107, 192 left, 197 right; Foto Jerry, Rio de Janeiro, 126; Marcel Gautherot, Rio de Janeiro, 33, 35, 64-65, 67, 129 bottom, 131 bottom; Gómez, Buenos Aires, 164, 192 center, 193 left, 195 center; Roger Halle, New York, 156, 157; G. E. Kidder Smith, New York, 19, 32; Arno Kikoler, 110; Laboratorio Palacios, Caracas, 117; J. Alex Langley, New York, 70, 71, 74, 75, 108; Paul Linder, Lima, 53; R. Maia & Franceschi, Rio de Janeiro, 170, 171; Rollie McKenna, New York, 22, 24, 25, 43 top, 47 bottom, 50, 52, 54, 55, 58, 59 top, 76, 81, 83, 91, 92-93, 95, 97, 100, 101, 105, 114, 115, 128, 130, 131 top, 134, 136, 137, 140, 141, 143, 151, 152, 153, 155, 159, 161, 162, 163, 172, 186, 187, 188 top, 196 left; C. U. Molina, Mexico, D.F., 15; Praisa, Mexico, D.F., 43 bottom; Walter Reuter, Mexico, D.F., 68; Armando Salas Portugal, Mexico, D.F., 46, 112, 113, 182, 184, 185; P. C. Scheier, São Paulo, 59 bottom, 119 bottom, 196 center; Servifoto, Havana, 194 center; J. Siqueira Silva, São Paulo, 119 top; Alexandre Smilg, São Paulo, 195 right; Grete Stern, 165; Ezra Stoller; Pictor, New York, 120; Elizabeth Timberman, Mexico, D.F., 47 top; Heinrich Ubbelohde-Doering: *Kunst im Reiche Der Inca*. Verlag Ernst Wasmuth, Tübingen, 1952, 14; Guillermo Zamora, Mexico, D.F., 104, 122, 123, 124, 178, 179, 181, 196 right.

This book has been printed in November, 1955, for the Trustees of the Museum of Modern Art by the John B. Watkins Company, New York

Museum of Modern Art Publications in Reprint

Max Ernst. 1961. William S. Lieberman

Fantastic Art, Dada, Surrealism. 1947. Barr; Hugnet

Feininger-Hartley. 1944. Schardt, Barr, and Wheeler

The Film Index: A Bibliography (Vol. 1, The Film as Art). 1941.

Five American Sculptors: Alexander Calder; The Sculpture of John B. Flannagan; Gaston Lachaise; The Sculpture of Elie Nadelman; The Sculpture of Jacques Lipchitz. 1935-1954. Sweeney; Miller, Zigrosser; Kirstein; Hope

Five European Sculptors: Naum Gabo—Antoine Pevsner; Wilhelm Lehmbruck— Aristide Maillol; Henry Moore. 1930-1948. Read, Olson, Chanin; Abbott; Sweeney

Four American Painters: George Caleb Bingham; Winslow Homer, Albert P. Ryder, Thomas Eakins. 1930-1935. Rogers, Musick, Pope; Mather, Burroughs, Goodrich

German Art of the Twentieth Century. 1957. Haftmann, Hentzen and Lieberman; Ritchie

Vincent van Gogh: A Monograph; A Bibliography. 1935, 1942. Barr; Brooks

Arshile Gorky. 1962. William C. Seitz

Hans Hofmann. 1963. William C. Seitz

Indian Art of the United States. 1941. Douglas and d'Harnoncourt

Introductions to Modern Design: What is Modern Design?; What is Modern Interior Design? 1950-1953. Edgar Kaufmann, Jr.

Paul Klee: Three Exhibitions: 1930; 1941; 1949. 1945-1949. Barr; J. Feininger, L. Feininger, Sweeney, Miller; Soby

Latin American Architecture Since 1945. 1955. Henry-Russell Hitchcock

Lautrec-Redon. 1931. Jere Abbott

Machine Art. 1934. Philip Johnson

John Marin. 1936. McBride, Hartley and Benson

Masters of Popular Painting. 1938. Cahill, Gauthier, Miller, Cassou, et al.

Matisse: His Art and His Public. 1951. Alfred H. Barr, Jr.

Joan Miró. 1941. James Johnson Sweeney

Modern Architecture in England. 1937. Hitchcock and Bauer

Modern Architecture: International Exhibition. 1932. Hitchcock, Johnson, Mumford; Barr

Modern German Painting and Sculpture. 1931. Alfred H. Barr, Jr.

Modigliani: Paintings, Drawings, Sculpture. 1951. James Thrall Soby

Claude Monet: Seasons and Moments. 1960. William C. Seitz

Edvard Munch; A Selection of His Prints From American Collections. 1957. William S. Lieberman

The New American Painting; As Shown in Eight European Countries, 1958-1959. 1959. Alfred H. Barr, Jr.

New Horizons in American Art. 1936. Holger Cahill

New Images of Man. 1959. Selz; Tillich

Organic Design in Home Furnishings. 1941. Eliot F. Noyes

Picasso: Fifty Years of His Art. 1946. Alfred H. Barr, Jr.

Prehistoric Rock Pictures in Europe and Africa. 1937. Frobenius and Fox

Diego Rivera. 1931. Frances Flynn Paine

Romantic Painting in America. 1943. Soby and Miller

Medardo Rosso. 1963. Margaret Scolari Barr

Mark Rothko. 1961. Peter Selz

Georges Roualt: Paintings and Prints. 1947. James Thrall Soby

Henri Rousseau. 1946. Daniel Catton Rich

Sculpture of the Twentieth Century. 1952. Andrew Carnduff Ritchie

Soutine. 1950. Monroe Wheeler

Yves Tanguy. 1955. James Thrall Soby

Tchelitchew: Paintings, Drawings. 1942. James Thrall Soby

Textiles and Ornaments of India. 1956. Jayakar and Irwin; Wheeler

**Three American Modernist Painters: Max Weber; Maurice Sterne; Stuart
Davis.** 1930-1945. Barr; Kallen; Sweeney

**Three American Romantic Painters: Charles Burchfield: Early Watercolors;
Florine Stettheimer; Franklin C. Watkins.** 1930-1950. Barr; McBride; Ritchie

**Three Painters of America: Charles Demuth; Charles Sheeler; Edward
Hopper.** 1933-1950. Ritchie; Williams; Barr and Burchfield

Twentieth-Century Italian Art. 1949. Soby and Barr

Twenty Centuries of Mexican Art. 1940

Edouard Vuillard. 1954. Andrew Carnduff Ritchie

The Bulletin of the Museum of Modern Art, 1933-1963. (7 vols.)

This reprinted edition was produced by the offset printing process. The text and plates were photographed separately from the original volume, and the plates rescreened. The paper and binding were selected to ensure the long life of this library grade edition.

DATE DUE

30 505 JOSTEN'S